A Walk Along
the Tracks

A WALK ALONG THE TRACKS

Hunter Davies

WEIDENFELD AND NICOLSON
LONDON

Contents

Illustrations

Dr Beeching in 1962 (*Keystone Press*)

Iron bridge under construction on the Great Central line, 1897 (*Leicestershire Museums*)

Pocklington School sports hall, formerly Pocklington Railway Station (*Pocklington School*)

Locomotives in the National Railway Museum, York (*Crown Copyright: National Railway Museum, York*)

Queen Victoria's saloon, used by the LNWR, on show at York (*Crown Copyright: National Railway Museum, York*)

Edward VIII and the Duke of York, at Ballater Station, 1936 (*Aberdeen Journals Ltd*)

Pitfodels Station on the old Deeside Railway (*Aberdeen Journals Ltd*)

Keswick Railway Station (*Peter W. Robinson*)

Hadlow Road Station on the Wirral Way (*Photo: Graham Hutt of Cheshire County Council*)

Railwaymen at St Briavels Station, 1923 (*Charles Fox*)

Charles Fox (*Hunter Davies*)

Tintern Station (*Hunter Davies*)

Monmouth Troy Station (*Hunter Davies*)

Christopher Somerville (*Hunter Davies*)

The old viaduct at Shepton Mallet (*Showerings Ltd*)

Alexandra Palace Station (*Lens of Sutton*)

Hunter Davies at Highgate Tunnel (*Frank Herrmann*)

The author and publishers are most grateful to the photographers and copyright owners for permission to reproduce the pictures.

The maps of the British railway system, in 1914, and in 1970, are reproduced by kind permission of the British Railways Board.

The maps at the beginning of each chapter were drawn by Patrick Leeson.

Introduction

When Dr Beeching took his axe
And gave BR those mighty whacks
A wondrous gift came free of tax
For all who love to walk the tracks.

THAT'S NOT SOME piece of ancient doggerel, left-over lines from
the sixties, forgotten folk lore from the Macmillan age. I just
made it up. This is an uplifting book, about a most marvellous
windfall which has come our way, a pleasure which every citizen
can go out and enjoy, though very few are yet aware of it. So I
thought I would begin with some bad light verse. You can sing
it if you like.

The closing of so many branch lines has been a tragedy and
although the mourning is still going on and blame and recri-
minations will continue and further lines will doubtless have
their death knell sounded, let us try to look on the brighter side.
We have suddenly been presented with more open space than
any planner in his wildest dreams could ever contemplate. Not
for centuries has so much 'virgin' land been available. There is
now almost as much disused railway land in Great Britain as
there is *used* railway land.

British Rail, when it came into existence in 1948, inherited
roughly 19,000 route miles. Today, the authorities have decided, in their wisdom, to make do with 11,000 miles. (By the
end of the 1980s, it is expected that another 3,000 miles will
have gone.) That means that out there, lying around somewhere, often overlooked, certainly undervalued, there are already 8,000 empty miles. Can any walker, any naturalist, any
lover of the countryside, any ornithologist, any botanist, any
social historian, any cyclist, any pony-rider and of course any
railway buff imagine anything more wonderful than having
8,000 empty miles to explore?

I'm getting slightly carried away, of course. Those 8,000 miles
are in corridors, and they're not necessarily all that empty.

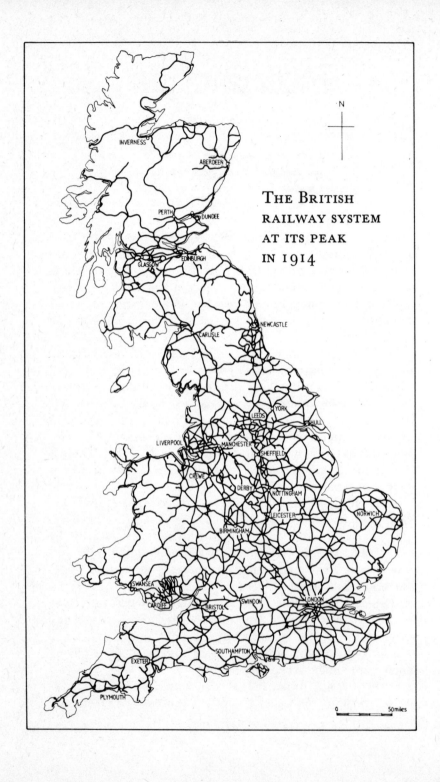

THE BRITISH
RAILWAY SYSTEM
AT ITS PEAK
IN 1914

N

INVERNESS

ABERDEEN

PERTH
DUNDEE

GLASGOW
EDINBURGH

CARLISLE

NEWCASTLE

LEEDS
YORK
HULL

LIVERPOOL
MANCHESTER
SHEFFIELD

CREWE

DERBY
NOTTINGHAM

LEICESTER
NORWICH

BIRMINGHAM

SWANSEA

CARDIFF
BRISTOL
SWINDON
LONDON

SOUTHAMPTON

EXETER

PLYMOUTH

0   50 miles

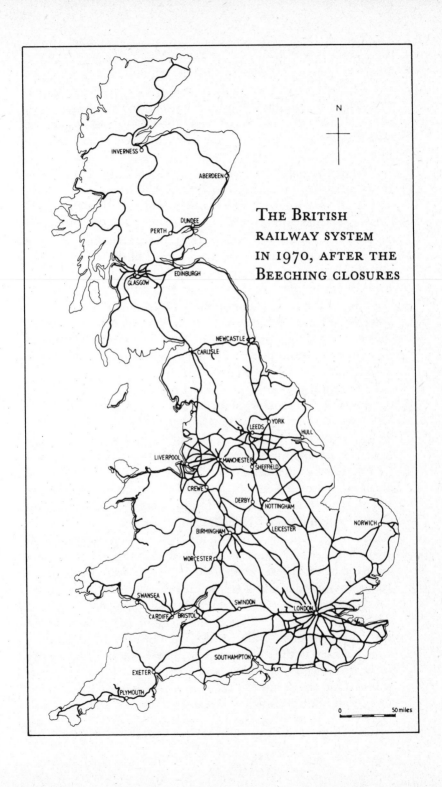

THE BRITISH RAILWAY SYSTEM IN 1970, AFTER THE BEECHING CLOSURES

Much of the land is highly inconveniently situated, exceedingly overgrown, littered with railway structures which are frighteningly costly to maintain, or even to flatten. And oh, the planning permissions, rules and regulations, bad buys and goodbyes. The problems, my goodness, the problems. We'll come to them later.

The fact remains that there does exist today 8,000 miles of disused railway lines. Think how marvellous it would have been to have had those 8,000 miles turned into interconnecting nation-wide walks and bridleways. British Rail has sold most of it piecemeal, which is a shame, though inevitable, but all is not lost. Local councils now own a great deal of this disused land, which in the end means you and me. Many enlightened councils have already made their stretches freely available, even cleaning them up and making them public walkways. No matter where you live in Britain, there's an old railway line nearby. Everyone, therefore, has a piece of their own local history, just waiting to be explored. Naturally, you might be trespassing, but that's another problem we'll discuss later.

I've spent a year walking disused railways. I had previously done a walking book on Hadrian's wall and then one on the Lake District but I don't think either of these walks gave me the *excitement* that walking an old railway track did. In every sense, you feel like an explorer. You don't have to be the slightest bit interested in the history of railways, although I am, to find pleasure in walking an old track. They're unique nature reserves. While farmers have been busy poisoning and carving up the surrounding fields for the last hundred years, the embankments of railways have been allowed to become preservation areas. You see and smell and touch flora and fauna that now hardly exist elsewhere. Even if, like me, you don't know much about botany or ornithology, you can't fail to be impressed.

I thought I'd discovered a virgin literary topic, not just virgin soil, when I started this book, but in the last year two books have appeared on a similar theme, each beautifully illustrated, though aimed at the railway public. There will be dozens more in the years to come. This is a new subject with endless possibilities. One day, I hope, a Pevsner or a Wainwright will come along and fully document all disused railways, though it will need an army of researchers, or a lifetime of love and patience, plus a large shelf to hold all the volumes which will result.

The only slight worry I have is that the subject, and the books, will become wholly part of railwayana. That is a huge and fascinating field but in recent years it has become very much a specialist technical market with the outsiders feeling rather excluded. Walks along old railways are walks for everyone. On my railway walks I've tried throughout to keep the general public in mind.

As in my previous walking books, I've devoted around fifty per cent of my time to people and events I came across along the way. I've used the old railway routes to have a look at life today rather than just the nuts and bolts, facts and figures; to make it a human book, about the flesh-and-blood people who now live where the navvies once toiled. I hope that armchair travellers will be amused and entertained, informed and perhaps inspired, as well as those who already know the delights of railway walking.

I carefully chose ten different old lines in different parts of the country to give the book a regional spread. I also tried to mix the converted with the neglected, the lines which are now like public parks and those where you need a machete before each stride. I'd never been to any of them before. I hope that you, in looking down the contents list to see the ones I've chosen, won't be put off by any strange sounding places. They're not meant for purely local consumption. I believe each one also has a national interest.

I've tried to build up a total picture as I've gone round the country, using each walk in turn to bring in a new element. The botanical surveys, for example, that I describe in the Deeside Line (chapter 4) have counterparts in all the walks. The row I relate in the Ally Pally section (chapter 10), about a preservation group's work to save the line, could have been repeated in almost every chapter, but I thought one was enough. By reading the chapters in sequence the major pleasures and problems of railway walking should become apparent. You can then put down the book, get out a pair of stout shoes, find an old map of your area, and go off to explore for yourself. I have probably considered only something in the region of five hundred miles of old railways in these ten walks, and even then I have concentrated on certain sections. I've left you 7,500 miles, some of which I've attempted to list in the Appendix. Happy walking.

HUNTER DAVIES
London NW5   1981

P.S. You won't, of course, do any trespassing, will you? I should hate to be responsible for encouraging anyone to think that all old railway lines are open to the public. Naturally, you'll write to BR in advance to find out the present owners and seek their permission. Should this slip your mind, take care to do no damage, to respect the countryside, and to avoid what is obviously private; and, when accosted, always apologise immediately . . .

1 🚂 Three Bridges to East Grinstead

A WALK IN COMMUTER COUNTRY AND A MEETING WITH A VERY IMPORTANT PERSON ...

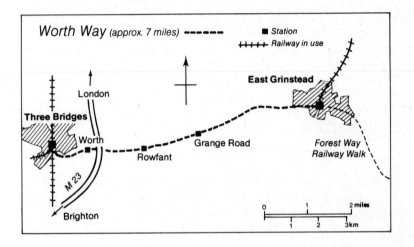

Worth Way (approx. 7 miles) ▪ Station — Railway in use

London
Three Bridges
Worth
Rowfant
Grange Road
East Grinstead
Forest Way Railway Walk
M 23
Brighton

0   1   2 miles
1   2   3km

I'D NEVER BEEN to London Bridge station before, which is strange, considering I've lived in London for over twenty years. I wasn't even quite sure where it was. People who come from the North of England tend to settle in the north of London and they tend to use the termini, like Euston, King's Cross and St Pancras, which serve the northern outposts of the provinces. Crossing the Thames, and going over to South London, is like going abroad. Southerners must feel the same.

Yet London Bridge is London's oldest railway terminus. It was opened on Wednesday, 14 December 1836, using land which cost £7,500 and had previously been a burial ground. It wasn't *much* of a railway, being only a three-and-a-half-mile stretch between London and Greenwich, but the London and Greenwich Railway Company was very proud of its massive viaduct, with 851 arches, which led into London Bridge station.

Today, it is amongst London's busiest stations with 150,000 passengers using it every day, most of them commuters from Kent and Sussex. The building was badly damaged during the last war but extensive rebuilding was completed in 1979 when an opening ceremony was performed by the Bishop of Southwark, Dr Stockwood, accompanied by the comedian Frankie Howerd (who was invited as a local boy).

I went in search of a cup of tea as I had time to kill before the 9.42 to Three Bridges. I'd been warned by the ticket man that under no circumstances could I use my cheap day return until that time. I passed a bar called the Oast House, in memory of the thousands of London hop-pickers who used this station in the old days, on their way to Kent.

Many of the commuters were still arriving, coming in from the suburbs in their neat suits, marching silently across the forecourt, as if in a daze, their minds elsewhere, their muscles performing in a dream, Kipps-like figures, all something in the City.

On the almost empty train, returning whence they had just

come, we sped past mythical names like Purley and Horley, mythical to me because I've never been quite sure if they existed, legendary places from the soft underbelly of South-East England.

I could have begun my railway walking with something wild and remote but I wanted to work my way geographically round the country. London is as good a place as any to start from. And in the Sussex commuter belt where I was going lives a Very Important Person whom I wanted to meet, someone of interest to all railway walkers.

I did at one time contemplate moving out and becoming a commuter myself, escaping to the green belt, to the fresh air and a chance to buy a cheap, attractive, modern house. I'm glad I didn't. Facts and fashions have changed so much these last twenty years. Those poor white-collars who elected to live thirty miles away, pleased to pay just £10 a year for a season ticket, now have to pay around £500 a year – and for fewer trains and more delays and endless life-sapping frustrations. The railways made them and now, sadly, the railways are ruining their lives, judging by the angry letters most evenings in the London *Standard*. The newspaper has even been running a Commuters' Club which helps to focus their grievances.

Three Bridges, one of the many commuter towns which the railway created, was just a dot on the map until 1855 when a branch line was opened, connecting it to East Grinstead. A village then grew up round the railway station, as it did at Haywards Heath and scores of other places. Alas, the seven-mile branch line from Three Bridges to East Grinstead was a cross-country connection, a lateral line, not a route in and out of London. Naturally, when the world changed for branch lines, it was one of those in 1966 which Dr Beeching deemed superfluous.

I came out of Three Bridges station and went first to buy an Ordnance Survey map. I already had a pamphlet produced by West Sussex Council on Worth Way – which is what they now call the old railway line – but I wanted more detailed information. Almost at the station entrance I found a bookshop: it was in semi-darkness, but there was a man inside who said yes, rather gruffly, he was open, and I asked for the local OS map. 'You want sheet 198,' he said at once. 'We haven't got it.'

I could see a large row of those familiar purple covers on a counter and asked if he minded if I looked through them, as people rarely put them back in the right order. 'I've already looked,' he said. I gently eased myself nearer, squinting down the row, murmuring apologies, and sure enough, there was a 198. I pulled it out triumphantly. He groaned, looked up at the ceiling, but allowed me to take it.

I couldn't find East Grinstead anywhere. I turned it over and worked out from the master plan that it was 187 I really wanted. 'We haven't got that either.' He was obviously pleased my little triumph had been ruined. He tried to bar my way this time from even looking at his maps.

'Do you mind?' he said. 'It *is* my day off.' I apologised profusely, but after all, he had said the shop was open, even though it now appeared that its speciality was not selling things. There was one 187 left. I grabbed it and thanked him. Luckily, I had £1.40 in exact change or there could have been a major diplomatic row.

I came out feeling pleased with myself, to find the heavens had opened and the sky was throwing itself down in a mad suicide bid. I sheltered under the bridge and got out my anorak and leggings. I was already wearing wellingtons, as the day had looked dark, but had in my rusksack a pair of clean shoes and socks. As I hoped to visit my Important Person at the end of this walk, I didn't want to stagger into his living room in muddy wellies.

I walked past a playing-field, following a wooden sign marked Worth Way, and soon picked up the old railway line itself. I was immediately in another world, deep in dense undergrowth, remote from semi-detached suburbia, though for a while to my right I could hear in the distance the occasional train on the main line, heading for London, some forty miles away.

Much of the Sussex countryside was once very like the old railway line is now, a mass of trees and bushes. They cut a lot down for charcoal from the fifteenth century onwards to smelt iron, though by the early nineteenth century the iron industry had moved north. When John Urpeth Rastrick first produced a scheme for this branch line, in 1845, it was probably still well wooded. It was the new commuter villages which finished off most of the remaining forests.

Mr Rastrick is an engineer well known in railway circles. He was a contemporary of George Stephenson's, though they were deadly rivals for a long time. Rastrick was one of two leading engineers of the day who had been called on by the Liverpool–Manchester company to decide whether their proposed railway should use stationary engines (fixed beside the track to pull wagons up inclines) or moving locomotives.

Rastrick and his colleague Walker went across to Darlington in 1828 to have a look at George's Stockton–Darlington railway which was using locomotives. One of their many damning statistics was that moving a ton of goods thirty miles by fixed engines cost 6.4 pence a mile while the cost of moving it by locomotives was 8.36. It makes one wonder how many other times in history cold statistics have ruined progress. George, a self-taught mechanic who hated all professional engineers, got his son Robert to prepare a counter-report. 'Rely upon it,' wrote Robert to a friend, 'locomotives shall not be cowardly given up. I will fight for them until the last.'

Rastrick and Walker, in their report, did admit that there were grounds for expecting some improvement in the performance of locomotives. The upshot, as all railway enthusiasts know, was the Rainhill Trials of 1829 when the directors decided once and for all to have a contest and find out what these newfangled locomotives could really do. Mr Rastrick was appointed one of the three judges – and he well and truly was made to eat his words when the *Rocket* startled the whole world. It's nice to realise that Rastrick himself saw the light and went on to become a successful engineer of locomotive railways.

His East Grinstead branch line, which was extended another nine miles to connect with Groombridge in 1866, was originally part of the London, Brighton and South Coast Railway. It was eventually eaten up by the Southern Railway Company in 1922 which in turn disappeared by 1948 when railways were being nationalised to become British Rail.

The most emotional year for every railway fan was 1968 when steam disappeared for ever, at least as far as British Rail is concerned. Since then, railways have become an art form and anything to do with the old railway companies is now a collector's item. Bands of enthusiasts have privately re-opened many old lines with enormous success, bringing back steam to their preserved lines.

One of the best known is the Bluebell Railway, just a few miles to the south of East Grinstead. It runs through some very pretty Sussex countryside, from Sheffield Park to Horsted Keynes, a distance of some five miles, and operates daily from Easter to October. (Details are in the BR timetable.) Spring is the time to try it out when the silver birch woods are full of bluebells.

The Worth Way has been equally beautifully preserved, but as a country walk. The rails and ballast have gone and the council have thoughtfully put down a new surface, some of it made of chalk which is what the original railway builders often used to line the embankments. For most of the way, the line passes over sandstone, but there are bands of clay. It's this mixed geological surface, with the addition of the chalk, that has made the flora and fauna so rich. On this little stretch of line, only six miles long (a mile has been lost with infilling), the experts have recorded 270 different plants, including the Cuckoo flower, the common spotted orchid and the guelder rose.

The animal life is known to be equally rich and varied. All day I kept a look out for kestrels and sparrow-hawks, as these big birds of prey are known to hunt the railway line, searching for small mammals, like mice and voles, but all I saw were two squirrels and a rabbit.

The third bridge I came to along the old track rather ruined the rural idyll. There was the most revolting smell, the source of which I eventually located in a sewage pipe, leading straight down on to the line. There were also piles of old mattresses and other junk lying around. You have to expect a bit of despoliation at bridges as people can so easily dump rubbish over the sides.

As on all railway lines, there is the tantalising switchback feeling of going up and down, one moment looking out across fields as the track appears to rise up, the next deep in a gorge, with embankments towering either side. In reality, you hardly ever rise or fall very much, especially in tame, gentle countryside like Sussex, as the engineers have smoothed out most bumps to accommodate the track.

It must have been a great boon to Rastrick and his fellow

engineers, back in the 1840s, when first surveying the line, to have such flat countryside. In the very early days, engineers often still used stationary engines as well as locomotives, as George and Robert Stephenson did, if they came to a hill too steep for their little locomotives.

I saw ahead of me what appeared to be a definite slope which I walked up slowly, wondering if a cutting had been filled in, and found my way ahead barred by a stout wooden fence. I climbed up to it, looked over, and there was the ultimate horror of the modern world for all walkers, a motorway. I don't know how I hadn't heard the noise. The deep undergrowth of the old railway must have cushioned it. It was the M23, along which motorists were hurling themselves south towards Brighton.

The rain was still coming down in sheets and there wasn't a great deal of traffic on the road, not compared with the M1 or the M6. There were no clues as to which way I should turn. Having been quite generous so far with their wooden notices, the council were now giving nothing away. I thought for a moment of trying to run across the motorway, but decided that the lightness of the traffic was deceptive. There were two pedestrian bridges some distance away, one to either side, and I decided to head for the nearer one, on the left. I could see clearly across the motorway where the line of the old railway had re-formed itself and was heading once more for East Grinstead, pretending the motorway had never happened.

As I crossed the bridge, I looked over for a brief moment, up and down the mad highway, which seemed about ten times as wide as my little railway. I wondered how many centuries it would be before walkers were tramping disused and overgrown motorways, looking for signs of motorway archaeology: the crumpled concrete bridges, rusted lane-closed symbols, white-on-blue dashes meaning an intersection is coming up, one bar equals a hundred yards, leading future industrial historians to the ancient Watford Gap Service Station and perhaps an un-eaten plate of chips and fried eggs, no longer edible of course, but identifiable by carbon dating. We know the Romans ate shell-fish on Hadrian's Wall, because they left the shells. Doubtless posterity will find equally good clues about us and our awful motorway eating habits.

Hadrian's Wall stood for four hundred years, which must be a record as a line of communication goes. The turnpikes lasted hardly at all, being overtaken by the canals and then the railways before they'd reached their peak. Why should motorways and the internal combustion engine last for ever? Nothing else has.

Once safely across the M23, I went along the other embankment and hit the old railway again. It turned out to be so overgrown I had to fight and kick my way through. Perhaps I had missed an entrance and this bit was private, left to go completely wild. I disturbed more birds and rabbits and insects and butterflies than in the whole journey so far. There was a mass flight ahead of me, a scurrying and screeching as I struggled to make progress. They'd presumably got used to the noise of the motorway over the years, but the sight and sound of a human being about to stumble over them must have been rather alarming.

Eventually, the way ahead cleared and I came to a broad, two-lane path, like a cart track, the best and broadest path I'd come across so far. Despite the rain, and several little ponds by the side of the track, it was good enough to cycle on.

I bashed on till I came to Rowfant station, the first halt for railway passengers after Three Bridges. The buildings are still there, including the station-master's house, the waiting-rooms and the platforms, all in excellent condition, considering they date back to 1855. The site announced the name Redland, the concrete firm. I looked around, hoping for somewhere to shelter, and found myself amongst a host of large yellow lorries, the sort used for white-lining the roads. On the ground were hundreds of criss-crossing white lines as if some crazy roadmen had been allowed to run wild. I suppose white-liners have got to practise white-lining somewhere.

I came back to the station building but failed to get in. It appeared not to be in use and the doors were padlocked, so I stood in a doorway sheltering from the rain, thanks to generous, overhanging carved eaves. The London, Brighton and South Coast Railway was noted for its handsome station buildings, as befitted the affluent commuters they were carrying. All the old railway companies had their individual architectural styles, with localised variations, as the companies tried to reflect the area, using local stones and flints. At a seaside resort, for example, they often gave their stations the appearance of a holiday-villa, with verandahs and shutters.

I looked around for any old railway signs, with no success, there were a couple of lamp-holders still fixed to the walls and the carved decorated boards on the gables and the dormers were all in good condition. I peered through one of the criss-cross lattice-work windows, very fancy and still intact, and could see what had been the booking office, painted dark green. It was empty, apart from a dozen or so green plastic venetian blinds.

Not long after leaving Rowfant station, I came across a mass of little red apples, scattered over my path like scarlet confetti. They were the size of crab apples, but looked tantalisingly sweet and juicy. Most trees on the Worth Way, as on all old railways, are self-sown, but apple trees don't sow themselves. Perhaps this tree had grown from a thrown-away apple core, which does sometimes happen, though their fruit is usually mushy and nasty. I took one bite, just to try them, and it was delicious. I ate half a dozen, then followed them with half a packet of rather soggy Polos which had lain in my anorak pocket all year. A simple lunch. One must eat off the land when one can. I suppose you *could* eat off railway tracks, if you knew what you were doing and could identify all the berries and plants and had a strong constitution. I felt a few sharp pains but put it down to my imagination.

The track led me suddenly into a brand-new housing estate, still being built. There was a new pub, amongst all the smart semi-detached houses, which I would have stopped at if the weather had been better and if I hadn't got my important personage to see. I didn't want to be late for him. He had taken long enough on the phone the day before to agree to being in when I called. I'd discovered by chance that he lived right beside the old East Grinstead branch line. He was certainly someone I didn't want to miss.

All the streets in the little estate were named after trees – Hazel Close and Rowan Walk and Alder Way. I'd seen lots of hazels and alders but not a rowan. A rowan tree, or mountain ash, is one tree I can identify. I hoped I hadn't been eating large red rowan berries by mistake.

The streets were deserted, as the rain was determined to make a day of it, but occasionally through a front window I could see a young mother sitting at an empty polished dining-room table, lost in dreams, slowly feeding a baby in its high chair. Far away at the front line, the husbands were fighting the good fight for differentials and luncheon vouchers and index-linked pensions.

I overtook a rather dashing young man walking slowly in the rain in a long overcoat and white clogs. He said 'Hello'. I told him I was walking the old railway line. 'Not the sort of thing I'd do,' he said. He kindly pointed out a short cut through the estate which took me straight on to the Worth Way again.

It was the first conversation I'd had all day. I managed my second very brief encounter a few minutes later. I asked directions from a lady on a bicycle riding along the tracks with a dog. The dog was wearing a mackintosh and was running breathlessly to keep up with his mistress. She said she'd been into East Grinstead to play squash. She waved her racquet at me, in case I didn't believe her, or to warn me off, then rode away.

Just before East Grinstead, I came to a modern concrete bridge completely covered in graffiti. I thought at first the Russians had arrived as I made out letters which looked like CCCP, written several times, then scored out. Finally, the unknown hand had managed CHESSEA and I realised that football supporters aren't the most literate of writers, especially when hanging over a bridge trying to write upside down.

Under the bridge, the lettering was much clearer. 'This IS the modern world,' declared one wall, rather elliptically. On another wall I read, 'Is there Life before Death?'

I got into East Grinstead just three hours after leaving Three Bridges. The Worth Way runs straight into a busy, working railway station, surrounded by the commuter cars, parked forlornly for the day, obedient animals, waiting for their masters' return. The old track continues east from East Grinstead, along what's called the Forest Way, but I had to change into my dry shoes, smarten myself up and find my way to Little Manor, home of the gentleman I was planning to meet. He'd said on the phone it was just a mile from the church, going south, a few hundred yards from the old railway line which he could see from his garden.

In the middle of East Grinstead they've recently converted the old railway line into a modern inner ring road, a deep curving road which takes you round the town centre. There was talk of calling the new road Beeching Cut, as there are high cuttings on either side, but the use of the word 'cut' was thought a bit too satirical. Instead, it is known officially as Beeching Way, which is very apt, in every way.

Perhaps you have already guessed the identity of my VIP, as East Grinstead has been the home of Lord Beeching for the last twenty-three years, ever since he himself, like thousands of others, decided it was a pleasant place to live, a handy train ride away from London. It's a mock-Tudor house in extensive grounds. Dr Beeching, as he then was, was a director of ICI when he bought it, and it was from here that he commuted to London by train for twelve years.

Lord Beeching turned out to be taller than I'd expected, which is strange as most well-known figures turn out smaller in real life. His moustache is still there, a gift for all the cartoonists of the sixties. Although his face has now disappeared from our screens and newspapers, his name lives on. Doing a Beeching has almost become a term in itself, fit for the Oxford dictionary, meaning vigorous pruning of dead branches, of any sort, in any business.

He turned out to be a lot jollier than he'd sounded on the phone, not at all unwilling to talk about his old railway days. He seemed resigned to, even amused by, the image we all still have of him. 'I suppose I'll always be looked upon as the axe man, but it was surgery, not mad chopping.'

Looking back, it is almost impossible now to believe he ever got away with it. Whether you approve or not – and most railway romantics doubtless still disapprove – it was a remarkable achievement. In just four years at British Rail, arriving as an outsider, he was responsible for closing over 6,000 miles of lines and cutting the establishment by 140,000 railwaymen.

He was born in 1913, the son of a journalist, and spent his boyhood at Maidstone in Kent. From the local grammar school he went to Imperial College, London, where he took a first in Physics and then a Ph.D. He became a research scientist, joining ICI in 1935 where he rose to become Technical Director. He was forty-seven when the Call came, and it all happened by chance. Macmillan's Government was setting up an Advisory Group to look at British Rail as it was losing so much money. They wanted suitable outsiders to join the committee, especially people with experience of some other big businesses. A gentleman from ICI was approached: he declined but in doing so recommended Richard Beeching, then unknown to the general public.

During the year that the group studied British Rail, it became clear to everyone, particularly Mr Marples, then the Minister of Transport, that Dr Beeching was proving to be the dominant member of the group, with the strongest and most articulate views on exactly what should be done with BR.

'The first problem was to find somebody to put the Group's recommendations into effect. If I'd been brighter, I should have seen what would happen next, but it was a surprise, and a shock, when Marples asked me to take over BR as Chairman. I did hesitate for a while. It wasn't the sort of job I would normally have chosen. It's always unpleasant to have to deal with an organisation in severe trouble and I knew I would have to face press and media exposure, which I'd never done before.'

The first shock-horror reaction in the press was his salary – £24,000 a year. This was 1961 and previous chairmen had only got around £8,000. It was thought in those days that bosses of nationalised firms should do it for the honour. What wasn't fully recognised at the time was that his ICI salary had already been £24,000. He was taking on a huge load of trouble, for no extra pay.

The second shock was the speed at which he brought out his first Report, announcing that the axe was about to fall. 'People didn't realise that for a whole year previously I'd had an opportunity to study BR in connection with the Advisory Group and the plans for a thoroughgoing investigation had already been prepared when I took over.

'Most senior railwaymen readily accepted my arrival and the approach which I explained to them. The proposals which emerged were unpleasant, but the majority recognised them as offering the only credible solution to the railways' problems. I was amused by the absurdities of outside reaction. Many politicians agreed with the plans but some of them were quick to object to closures in their own constituencies.'

But didn't he have any feelings for the services in remote areas which would have to be killed?

'The trains were empty,' he replied flatly, seeing no reason to add anything else. To him the logic, then and now, is irrefutable.

'I know many railway people are sentimental about running railways. They love doing it and, like the public, they don't work out cause and effect. The public weren't using these branch lines, but they wanted them *in case* they ever should. In that case, they should *pay* to keep them open. Why should we use tax-payers' money and subsidise their desire for belt and braces?

'Several resort towns on the coast made special pleas to have uneconomic lines continued because of their dependence on them for holiday traffic. This dependence was never very real and the thought of paying soon had a salutary effect. I think it was in the case of Whitby I said they would need to find about £50,000 a year to cover our losses – and they decided it wasn't worth it.

'The reason why the branch lines were so little used was that people were going by car. I've forgotten the figures now, as it's over fifteen years ago, but there were some lines where a total of only ten people a day travelled on ten trains. It was madness.

'When there was an uproar about the proposed closure of the Kyle of Lochalsh service a long-service railwayman said to me, "I am sorry to have to say it, but even in summer when the Kyle is swarming with people, they have nearly all come by car."'

Looking back, he is more than willing to take *credit* for the cuts. He can't understand anyone *blaming* him for them. 'It is never kindness to perpetuate a state of decay. You are only prolonging the agony.'

He's slightly disappointed, though, that many people forget the creative things that started during his four years, such as the concentration of the present Inter-City routes and the ra-tionalisation of freight traffic movement. 'The railways depend on freight – it's their most profitable department, far more than passengers. I don't know the figure today, but I'm sure it is still true. In looking at the wagon fleets we found what the average speed of wagons was between terminals. Can you guess? How fast do you think a normal wagon went, from loading to un- loading?' I guessed twenty-five miles an hour.

'Half a mile per hour! They were spending most of their time being marshalled. The marshalling system, which was de- veloped as a clever means of linking any point on the system with any other, had become imposed on *all* traffic. As a result there were large and unpredictable delays in transit lanes for *all* wagons.

'The system was that everything went into marshalling yards at various points round the country with an average of about four and a half marshallings per transit. We set out to improve the amount of freight that was carried by through movement, i.e. without marshalling. In those days it was about ten per cent. Today eighty per cent of the wagons go direct.

'We also resolved the age-old question of whether apparent shortage of wagons at the collieries was due to congestion caused by excessive numbers in circulation, or to a genuine shortage in numbers. We cut the number by fifty per cent and availability improved. Now the number has been halved again by greater movement.'

He never set out with special targets, such as to save £20m, or to cut by exactly ten per cent. He has never started out with figures. They come at the end, not the beginning. He simply looks in great detail at everything, then cuts all the dead wood. Duplication of services particularly offended him. 'There were five lines across the Pennines, from Merseyside to Humberside. Three ways of getting from London to the West Country. Two ways from London to Birmingham. Naturally, if you live in Leamington Spa and the London–Birmingham train doesn't stop there any more you're a bit upset, but the vast majority of people on that train want to go direct London–Birmingham. Leamington Spa doesn't matter to them. One London–Bir- mingham service could easily be made to carry the whole of the traffic between the two cities.

'We have today some 8,000 miles of trunk railway – and they carry about ten per cent of the nation's trunk freight, while

3,000 miles of roads carry the other ninety per cent. Something is still wrong. We've got too many lines.'

Lord Beeching – he was created a Life Peer in 1965 — is very fond of throwing out such startling facts and figures. Even now, in his retirement, he continually reels them off, so goodness knows what he must have been like to argue with, back in the sixties, when he was at his height and with all the up-to-date figures at his fingertips.

'In 1830 there was one small area of the world where ninety per cent of the world's shipping was being built. Where was it?'

I said 'Pass.' The answer, he said, give or take a few percentages, was the eastern seaboard of the United States, in particular the Hudson river. Before that, the ships of the day had been built in Europe using hardwood. The need to build quickly and cheaply for the China trade led to the use of softwoods and as a result the world's ship-building crossed the Atlantic to be near the supply of North America's softwoods.

'In 1880, eighty per cent of the world's ships were being built by the side of another river. Which was it?'

I got it right this time. The Clyde.

'Correct. The world was now building iron ships, not softwood ones, and the iron and steel industry was on the Clyde. In fifty years, a huge industry had crossed the Atlantic twice. The basic lesson is absolutely clear. Skill is very mobile. There is no such thing as inherent skills.

'Twenty-five years ago everyone in Britain was reassuring themselves by saying "Ah yes, but we've got the skills." The Japanese, so everyone said, were just copiers. No need to worry about them ...

'Our supposed monopoly in skills in the end has proved fugitive. We were in the vanguard with semi-conductor research — but where's the silicon chip industry? Certainly not here.

'I suppose I have become more cynical as I get older, but this is understandable, natural and altogether proper. It would be a pity, after all, to be stupid enough not to learn from one's experience of life. It shows that human folly is very repetitive.'

He left British Rail after four years, by which time he'd cut the annual loss from £180m to £120m and closed a third of Britain's 18,000 railway miles.

'An astonishing amount was done, and it was more than I expected, but there was still a lot to do. I like to think my first Report, on the reshaping of British Railways, was the most thoroughgoing study of a problem of that size and kind which had ever been done.

'Because of railway enthusiasm, it was something of a best seller. The first issue was about 20,000 but it had to be reprinted and I believe the final total was around 50,000.'

Then came the second Report, the one which moved on to the plan for the rationalisation of the main lines.

The Tory Government had fallen by this time and Mr Marples, Dr Beeching's staunch supporter, was replaced by the Socialist Minister of Transport, Tom Fraser.

'The new Government wanted to pretend that they had plans of their own, although it soon became apparent that they did not and the new Minister told us not to publish the new report. I had to tell him that it was within my authority to decide and that I proposed to do so in order that the work would never be lost to sight. He said that the Government wouldn't allow HMSO to publish it. That was of no importance. We just made our own arrangements for publication.'

Harold Wilson, the Prime Minister, then asked Dr Beeching, rather surprisingly, to prepare an overall transport plan for the country, but Dr Beeching finally had to refuse because of the conditions attached to the way in which it was to be done.

'I found it ironical that my plans had been criticised by the Labour Party in opposition, because they did not conform with an overall plan for transport, and then to be asked to prepare such a plan by the same party when it came to power.'

He does not regard the running of the railways, or any other form of transport, as appropriate ground for party political squabbling. For that reason he delayed his resignation for a year after the change of government, but then he returned to ICI, as he had always intended to do.

He agrees that, from some points of view, he would have preferred to have stayed longer to implement the Report on the Rationalisation of the Trunk Routes, but, as he says, there's a limit to the extent to which a man can be expected to bang his head against a wall.

He went back to ICI, by whom he'd only been seconded to BR. Then, after three years, he became chairman of the Royal Commission on Assizes. 'You might enjoy reading the report. I wrote most of it and I am pleased to be told that it is exceptionally readable. All the recommendations were implemented. I don't think any Royal Commission has had a one hundred per cent score before, or since.'

Then he became chairman of Redland, the large building materials organisation. He was also chairman of Furness Withey for a time. He retired two years ago from active full-time work, after a period of poor health. Today he is a director of just two companies, Redland and Lloyd's Bank.

He spends most of his time at home in East Grinstead, reading thrillers for fun, avoiding listening to the news on the radio as he says it's all too depressing, and brooding upon the state of the universe. This latter activity is perfectly serious. 'I was a physicist once, forty years ago, and I do literally sit and think for hours about the cosmos. It's rather far-out science and would take a long time to explain . . .'

I changed the subject back to railways, especially the disused one he could see from his garden. He has walked bits of it, and enjoyed it, as it's a prettily wooded walk, but he can see no attraction in its railways associations. 'Why should I have romantic feelings about it? I can be moved if I see a battleship at sea, and have been, but I would never think of wanting to study them. I can't understand passionate railway nostalgia. It's now a mania which is rife throughout the world at large.'

At sixty-six, in reasonable physical health again, and with all his mental faculties obviously in good logical order, would he Answer if the Call came once again?

'It would have to be something substantial.' he replied, after a long pause. 'Yes, I would consider it, although it might be unwise of me.

'Despite all the aggravation, I suppose my time with the railways was the most exciting and stimulating time in my life. I was pitched into the limelight when nobody knew I existed before, then as far as most people were concerned, I returned to the darkness afterwards. It was in many ways just another job. At forty-eight, I'd already specialised in problem-solving which is what it always amounts to. I don't look upon myself as ruthless. I do what is in the best interest of everyone. I suppose my greatest disappointment is that I hoped that our treatment of the railway problem would set an example. I hoped that others would deal with other major national problems in the same rigorously logical way. It is rather sad that they don't. British Steel, British Leyland and the National Health Service all call out for that kind of treatment.'

He thinks the only thing to do with British Rail now is to rationalise the main lines, in the way he suggested in his second Report.

'Nearly all people are in favour of growth but few of them are equally ready to recognise that growth and decay go together. In the same way, they favour rationalisation, but don't want to pay the price of redundancy. Naturally, unions are concerned about loss of jobs, and all too often they oppose the very changes which are necessary to ensure the future health of industry and the future well-being of their members. The best you can do is adjust firmly and continually to the developing situation on the basis of the best possible market assessment.

'Yes, I might consider having one more go, if I were to be asked.'

Lady Beeching, who had kindly provided tea during her husband's dissertation, smiled but made no comment when I asked her if she would like her husband back on the firing line. I took that to mean that her husband would make up his own mind. Before I left, she took me me into another room to let me see what she calls the Cartoon Corner. She had arranged on some shelves the originals of many of the sixties cartoons, by people like Jon and Cummings. In one there's a grotesque figure of Beeching, panting down an empty platform while behind him two railwaymen are talking. 'I've told him the wrong platform.' She thought all of them were very funny.

She got my wet rucksack and things from the boiler room, now completely dry. 'Mr Marples always arrived with a rucksack. You're the first one since him.'

2 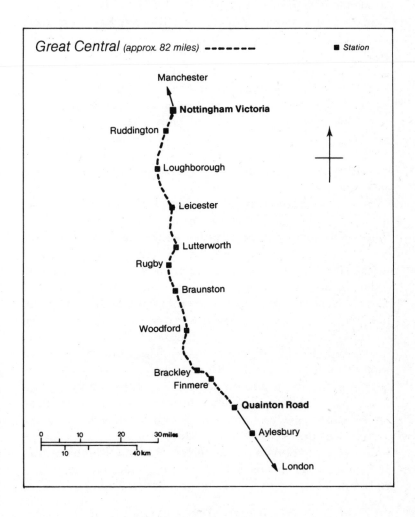 London and Leicester: on the trail of the Railway Ramblers

THE GREAT CENTRAL RAILWAY

Great Central (approx. 82 miles) ------- ■ Station

Manchester

■ **Nottingham Victoria**

Ruddington ■

■ Loughborough

■ Leicester

■ Lutterworth
Rugby ■

■ Braunston

Woodford ■

Brackley ■
Finmere ■

■ **Quainton Road**

■ Aylesbury

London

0   10   20   30 miles

10   40 km

THE BUILDING WAS small and new with no distinguishing features, about as architecturally interesting as an electricity sub-station. It was in the wasteland behind King's Cross, an anonymous blob in an anonymous street. There appeared to be no windows and no names on the blank front door, just a handwritten note pinned to one side, 'Railway Ramblers: Ring lower bell.' It could have been a cover for anything, or nothing at all.

A young man with an old-fashioned hairstyle, long but swept back like the pre-war literati, came to the door and led me upstairs. The meeting was just beginning. Fourteen members were already present for the second annual general meeting. He took me into a room, hired for the day, which looked like a changing room, with metal lockers all around. I recognized a framed poster on the wall, one I have at home, showing the steamboat *Gondola* on Coniston.

The bearded secretary, Nigel Willis, had just begun reading through the minutes of the last meeting. I looked around at the fourteen members, all men, sitting either side of a long trestle table. They all appeared so calm, so ordinary, so grey, yet I already knew that these gentlemen were pioneers, people of strong feelings and emotions. Before going on my next walk, I had decided to meet some of the enthusiasts in the same field.

Little did Dr Beeching know what he had unleashed when he closed all those thousands of miles of railway lines. Out of death and decay a different organism has grown up. It's a modest upsurge so far, but with strong shoots, tentacles now beginning to take a grip on many parts of the country.

Railway Ramblers, for such is their title, should really make Dr Beeching their patron saint, though it would be an ironic gesture, for they all feel a certain sadness in their breasts for the loss of so many railways. Nonetheless, Railway Ramblers have as their passion in life the love of rambling along old and disused railways.

Mr Willis, reading out apologies for absence, moved to the accounts. He said they'd spent a total of £223.59 during the year, which put them in debit by £9.73. There were no comments. He talked slowly in a strong Midlands accent. The only other noise was the occasional rustling of a plastic wrapper as the young man who had let· me in steadily fed himself from some packets of biscuits he'd laid out neatly in front of him on the table, little treats to get him through the day.

There was some momentary excitement when Mr Willis announced that their membership was now 127. A noisy discussion ensued when one member added up the individual totals, region by region, and made it 117 – London and the South, 36 members, Midlands 30, North 26, East 18, South-West 9, Scotland 6, West Indies 1, USA 1. Mr Willis said he was sure it was 127. No, no, said the member who had interrupted, Tony Field from Kent, who is the London and South-East area organiser, he made it 117. Look, he said to the member on his left, check my figures. Mr Willis said they'd better get on. He'd work on the figures later. Oh, heck, sorry, blurted out Mr Field. I've added up wrong. It *is* 127.

Mr Willis gave a quiet smile. He's a tall, rather schoolmasterly figure, an estimator for a Leicester roofing contractor. He carried on resolutely with his agenda, firmly getting through all the business. Everyone was in favour of raising the subscription from £1 a year to £1.50. They agreed that their little magazine, *Ramblings*, should from now on be quarterly not bi-monthly to save money.

There was some discussion about giving out membership cards. One member said a card would be a great help when you trespassed, showing a farmer that you weren't a vandal but a genuine old railways enthusiast. Flashing an identity card would immediately appease most farmers and private owners. 'What happens if you meet the farmer's dog?' There was a pause for a split second, enough for it to sink in that someone had made a joke. Then everyone laughed.

It hadn't so far been a meeting with much levity. It was a cold, grey January day with a hint of snow in the air and the room was hardly warmer than the windy streets of King's Cross outside. Several members had been up since dawn and had travelled long distances, mostly in buses to save money.

Plans were made to go on a railway ramble in Wales, staying at a youth hostel. It was hoped area reps would try to organise more local get-togethers, to visit neighbouring areas and investigate the old railway lines they'd discovered.

We all broke for lunch and trooped across the road to a pub which was empty, being Saturday, except for a few unshaven Irish gentlemen leaning on the bar and talking to the barmaid, who was also Irish. No hot meals today, love, only during the week, so all fifteen of us ordered ploughman's lunches and pints of beer.

Nigel Willis has always been interested in railways. He had been walking disused lines around Leicester with a friend for several years, till the friend gave up. It was in an effort to find someone to share his hobby that in 1978 he put a little advert in *Railway Magazine*. To his intense pleasure, he got 29 replies and decided to form Railway Ramblers. Their first ever meeting was held in January 1979 when 27 members turned up. He was terribly pleased that in only one year of existence they had jumped from 29 to 127 members, but he worried about the year ahead. Would people renew their original subscription? Would people actually *do* things, not just join? Would apathy set in, as so often happens with little clubs, after the initial burst of enthusiasm?

'Oh, I have no worries,' said a gentleman beside me, who said he worked for the Midland Bank. On closer inspection he wasn't so nondescript or grey in appearance, and neither was anyone else, once I got to know them individually. It was only in the mass that they gave that impression. He was carrying a dark leather handbag and wore a jaunty little denim cap. 'Oh, no. You see it's nostalgia. We'll easily get more members.'

Nigel Willis wasn't so sure, which was why he'd resisted some suggestions to put the subs up even higher. Keep it small, he thinks, and you won't lose people. He knew already that most people were members of other clubs, like the Model Railway Society, the Ramblers, the YHA and local railway organisations. If people decided to cut down and economise, Railway Ramblers as the newest arrival might go.

He was telling a couple of members how he'd recently bought a signal-box. He'd seen it over a year ago beside a disused line in Lincolnshire, while visiting relations. He took photographs, as he always does when he sees some railwayana. A year later, to his surprise, it was still there. He found the owner, a retired signalman, who didn't want it at the bottom of his garden any more, and offered him £30, agreeing to dismantle and take it away at his own expense. He borrowed a lorry, got a friend to help, and in a day they'd taken it down and brought it the ninety miles back to Leicester. It's now in Nigel's garage, while he waits for the better weather and works out how he can put together all the bricks and wood in his back garden.

A young man with a rather red face and country complexion said he'd walked sixty different disused railways, on his own, long before he heard about the existence of Railway Ramblers.

'I keep an eye out for them when I'm on a bus ride. If you're quick, you can spot them. I make a note, then go back later and explore.'

He had a pile of carefully written notes, which he handed to Nigel, humble offerings for the next issue of *Ramblings* magazine. Nigel already has enough railway rambles to keep him going for a year, but he accepted them gratefully.

The members include clerks, lorry drivers, teachers, doctors and one vicar. Mr Willis thinks they're all attracted by much the same sort of things which attract him.

'Firstly, there's the old railway associations. Then it's the wild life. And thirdly, there's an air of mystery in walking an old line. You don't know what you'll come across next. Come to Leicester and see what we've got ...'

Having joined the Railway Ramblers, and bought my little badge to prove it, I made plans after the meeting to go up to Leicester and join Nigel, a real expert, in walking an old railway, instead of just stumbling along in my own way, doubtless missing many of the treasures.

Railway fans, whether they walk disused railways, clean disused engines, work for steam preservation companies or run railway modelling societies, can roughly be divided into two sorts. The first variety, which is by far the bigger, is the

Statistician. They are obsessed by facts and figures and their knowledge is staggering. They can argue for hours about wheel bases, cylinders, boiler pressure, diameters of driving wheels. Their main pleasure seems to be in acquiring more and more details of a smaller and smaller section of their hobby. They're all lovely people, helpful and kind, will go out of their way and do anything for you, but once you show a passing interest, all their pent-up knowledge comes flooding out and they're hard to stop.

The other, and smaller variety of railway fan is the Romantic. I'm one of those. I'm interested in almost anything to do with steam railways, but I know very little about them. I collect railway stamps, for example. But when I look at a stamp, I decide whether it's pretty or not, rather than count the number of wheels on the engine. I'm fascinated by the life of George Stephenson but I don't understand how *Rocket* worked. I can make a fairly good guess at the age of a locomotive, and if the colour is green I might even have a stab at the railway company, but I could never give you its classification, its name or number, gender or tender. I'm in it for the nostalgia, the sounds, the smells, the visual beauty, as well as the history and the industrial architecture. Sir John Betjeman, our leading Railway Romantic, knows very little about flanges or fireboxes. He just loves railways.

The big thing about rambling old railways is that you don't *need* any technical knowledge. They're everywhere, and anyone, with a bit of elementary map-reading, can find them. They're simply country walks, open to all, though of a very special kind. It is indeed an extra pleasure to think of the long-gone steam engines, puffing up the same slopes, and to admire the railway artefacts left behind, but it's not necessary to know everything about the multifarious branch lines and complicated connecting links that once were all around, or the different railway companies all competing for business, or how many up-line express trains used this line or that on a winter Sunday in 1936. I leave all that to people like Nigel Willis, though it's certainly a bonus to have such a person around when walking an old line.

He was in the garden of his semi-detached house in the Aynstey Lane area of Leicester, not far from the speedway track. It's a modest little garden, but Nigel has some very grandiose ideas for it. All I could see were great piles of mud and deep trenches, pipes lying everywhere, planks over holes in the ground. In one corner there was a clue to his ultimate aim, several yards of a model railway track. His final solution for his garden is to turn it over completely into a $3\frac{1}{2}''$ gauge railway, over fifty yards long.

He has a Hornby steam-driven model of *Rocket*, running on butane gas, which will lead his train round and round the garden. He hopes one day to have a smaller gauge railway alongside the same circuit. Eventually, when both lines are finished, he'll have model houses, model stations and model factories. The plans are all drawn. The trenches are dug. All it will take, he thinks, is twenty-five years to finish it off.

His wife Libby is amused rather than horrified by his devotion. 'We were never much interested in gardening,' she says, watching her whole back garden disappearing. She shares his interest in railways and is pleased when he manages to turn all their holidays into railway rambles, along with their three young children. His ambition is to walk at least one disused railway in every county in England. They were going to Devon and Cornwall for their summer holidays, hoping to take in two old railway lines.

She's a secretary at Leicester University and types out all the material for *Ramblings*. She was quite pleased that Nigel, since I met him in London, had decided to sell his signal box. He tried to take me into the garage to see it, but we failed to get in. There's not much you can do with a pile of old planks and a load of old bricks, unless you actually build something, and Nigel is too busy elsewhere.

We set off at last on our walk, down a stretch of the nearby Great Central Railway, a line which Nigel himself used before it closed. Almost every old railway company has its own mythology, but in the books I'd been reading, the Great Central caused more weeping and wailing on its demise in 1966 than a great many others. It was, after all, a main line and, as we know Dr Beeching didn't manage to kill as many of those as he would have liked.

It was the last of the main lines to be built – and the first to die. It connected Manchester with London, via Sheffield,

[25]

Nottingham, Leicester, Rugby and Aylesbury, a route that even at the time wasn't strictly necessary, which was why it was so late in being built.

Two rival companies, the London and North Western and the Midland, had been running similar routes for fifty years before the idea of the Great Central came into the mind of Sir Edward Watkin, one of the great railway promoters of the late nineteenth century. He was already chairman of the Manchester, Sheffield and Lincolnshire and also of the Metropolitan in London, and naturally wanted to link the two and have his own direct route to London from Manchester, instead of using either of his rivals' services. Naturally, the LNWR and the Midland opposed the plans for the new line, and managed to wreck the initial stages of the necessary bills through Parliament, but permission was eventually obtained and the line was opened in 1897, when the Manchester, Sheffield and Lincolnshire changed its name to become the Great Central.

They had high hopes of catching a lot of the coal trade in the Midlands, particularly around Leicester, at the same time providing a very fast passenger service. They failed with the heavy traffic, but their passenger service became legendary. They had spent a fortune on the new line, over £6 million, which included costly tunnels on the last two miles into Marylebone, partly under Lord's cricket ground.

The Great Central was built with an eye to speed, raising the line whenever possible in order to eliminate the need for level crossings – in fact they managed with only one between Manchester and London. They went for straight lines, with the minimum of gradient, even when it meant massive earth-moving operations. They also had an eye to the future, keeping the embankments well back and building three-arch bridges, one of the many distinctive features of the Great Central. Their plan was one day to have four tracks, two up and two down, but they never managed it. Today's walkers now get the benefit of all their ambitions, being left with such a broad and straight pathway to ramble along.

We joined the line at Aylestone, on the south edge of the city, parking the car beside a rather garish bingo hall, with an enormous car park in front, and clambered up the embankment.

At road level, the area had seemed the usual urban sprawl, cramped and complicated little streets and odd rows of houses. Up on the line, it was like suddenly being in the Wild West. The line stretched south, straight as a die, into infinity, across what seemed like wide open plains.

To the right, we soon picked up the canal, the Grand Union, and a very attractive humped-back bridge, once used by pack-horses. Nigel had brought his camera to photograph the lock-keeper's house, which he remembered from his last visit, but it was empty and vandalised. He took the photo, nevertheless.

Later on, his camera came out again when we arrived at an old cast-iron boundary post. It marks the boundary of the Borough of Leicester and the Parish of Lubbes Thorpe. It's a handsome bit of decorated ironwork, triangular shaped, like a tube of Toblerone chocolate, with the distinctive Wyvern dragon, from Leicester's coat of arms, on top. The date said 1891, which seemed strange, as the railway wasn't opened till 1897. Had it been there, just by chance, exactly on the embankment, or had it been moved by the navvies? Nigel wasn't sure.

Another of the distinctive features of the Great Central is the use of blue brick, on bridges and on viaducts. There were several viaducts through Leicester, to keep the trains on the straight and the quick, but most of them have now been taken down. You can still see a few, hanging in mid-air, their middles eaten away, as if a giant has been going round, gobbling up the juicy bits. Nigel keeps an eye on the dismantling, taking photographs where possible and pocketing the odd blue brick. From a distance, the blue bricks look very stark, flat and boring, lacking the warmth of red brick, but Nigel loves every one of them. As he is in the building trade, he knows a good brick when he sees one.

'They come from Staffordshire, the blue bricks, and they're really solid. When they've taken these viaducts and bridges down, you find not one brick has moved. Blue bricks are fired very hard, much longer than normal red bricks, which puts the price up. They don't weather or wear or crumble. But they're very expensive, three times the price of ordinary bricks. That's why today they're normally only used in foundations, up to the damp course. They're also water-resistant.

[27]

'If you look carefully, you'll see they're not just blue – there are other shades in them, yellows and reds. I think they look beautiful. That's one of the things about walking old railways. You come to take a greater interest in all buildings. You start looking at ordinary houses in a different light, admiring little things. I can now see that architecturally there really is very little of interest in the city of Leicester, apart from industrial buildings like the gas works and a few factories.'

We passed many bridges on our walk, and I admired them all. I could see that the blue bricks hadn't moved or worn at all. Most of the bridges have lattice-work sides, made of strips of iron, another feature of the Great Central. Nigel has got a piece of Great Central lattice-work at home, another memory of happier days.

North of Leicester, there is a preserved stretch of the old Great Central, between Loughborough and Rothley, about five miles, which is run by a steam preservation society, one of the many which have sprung up all round Britain since the end of steam. This stretch of line goes across the Swithland viaduct and is a great tourist attraction, It's called the Great Central Railway (1976) Ltd and its headquarters are in the Loughborough Central station.

You can't actually walk through Leicester on the old line without trespassing, but south of Leicester, as I was beginning to see, you can walk for ever, well, for a very long way. Nigel has previously done it, walking over sixty miles on the old track, all the way to Aylesbury, with only one interruption, a short break for a gypsum works. It must be one of the longest un-impeded stretches of old railway line in the whole of Britain. It goes through some fine countryside near Charwelton and Cul-worth, but there is a stretch where you have to walk side by side with the M1, which doesn't sound much fun. 'It hardly bothered me. I was so busy looking at the old tracks, but I got some funny looks from motorists going past me, just a few yards away.

'The arrival of the car was one of the things which helped to kill the line. Financially it never became an established line, not enough to rival the Midland, and its birth at the turn of the century almost coincided with the birth of motor cars.'

We came to a filled-in bridge, which looked rather horrible, with debris spewed out nearby, part of a dumping ground for a brick factory by the look of it, but once over that, the line stretched neatly ahead again. A girl on a pony kindly agreed to take our photograph and Nigel handed her his camera. She said there was quite a bit of pony-trekking on the line. There was nowhere else near Leicester to exercise ponies, unless you owned your own fields. (The photograph didn't come out.)

Nigel got rather excited as we approached Whetstone station, pointing out bridge number 398 with its number still in place, just before the entrance. You had to climb up, through an archway in the bridge, to reach the station. Like the rest of the line, it sits high in the air, master of all it surveys. The ground has now been levelled, as flat as a huge football pitch, not a building in sight. The last time he was there one of the railway warehouses was still standing. All we could find was a low wall and a goods bay with the remains of the buffer stops. Amongst the overgrown grass and bracken nearby we found what looked like the original cast-iron buffers, but they were too heavy to move.

We stood silently, with Nigel remembering times past. The ground had been flattened so recently it looked like the beginning of an architectural dig. Perhaps one day the site will be excavated and people will try to work out where the station-master's house once stood, or the ticket office, or lavatories. Such excavations are already happening in some parts of the country, such as Edge Hill station in Liverpool.

There's a good picture of Whetstone station in its heyday in a book about the Great Central, by Colin Walker, *Main Line Lament*, which has many fine pictures of the line in its last ten years. Like most books on railways, which are mainly produced by Romantics, the writing often bursts into purple prose, humanising the engines. Great Central trains don't just run along the line but 'pull away majestically ... climb splendidly ... whisk confidently ... arrive nonchalantly ... make a vigorous exit'. Even the insides are glamorised. 'How magnificent those large, power-packed Gresley boilers looked when softly illuminated at night.' The drivers of the final trains are always giving sad waves, or proud glances. 'The camera catches Driver

George Evinson looking admiringly down the boiler of this V2 which is reflecting the morning sunshine.'

The Great Central did have a lot to be proud of. They really did beat their rivals for speed. According to a 1920 timetable, they were faster than the LNWR from London to Rugby (98 minutes compared with 100 minutes) and beat the Midland to Leicester (116 minutes compared with 120 minutes). Great Central drivers were allowed only 25 minutes to do the 23.5 mile stretch between Leicester and Nottingham, but often managed it in even time, much to the amazement of bystanders and even visiting railwaymen, used to the sedater ways of other companies. It was normal to see Great Central trains approach the viaducts into Nottingham and Leicester at over 60 mph, with only a mile to go before the station. The drivers were so used to their engines, and the straight line, that speeds of over 80 mph were common.

In 1920 there were nine express trains from London to Nottingham (four with restaurant cars) and eight in the reverse direction, all going at very fast speeds. There were surprisingly few bad accidents, though there was a famous one on 23 December 1904 when a driver took the curve into Aylesbury station rather too quickly. It was a parcels train, with Christmas post. Nobody was killed but a load of Christmas puddings were scattered all over the track, quickly to disappear when the word went round.

When the GCR was taken over by the London and North Eastern Railway in 1923 – the period when all the smaller companies were merged into the big four – its reputation for having the best and the fastest engines was continued when they were given Gresley's A3 Pacifics, considered the best of the day.

Great Central drivers rarely went in for double heading – using two engines at the front to pull a train up steep inclines – but relied on one engine, and their own expertise, plus of course the advantages of a well-laid track and gentle gradients.

We stood on a long blue-brick viaduct just outside Whetstone and Nigel pointed out the little square openings at various points along the viaduct, hiding places where track men could take refuge should they be on the viaduct when a Great Central express flew past them at 80 mph, threatening to blow them into the river or canal.

We walked on as far as the M1, but I couldn't face seeing or hearing the motorway, far less walking beside it, so we came back to Leicester.

The end began in 1966 when they started to close most of the Great Central stations and reduced the number of trains. Steam had already gone by then, but a diesel service of sorts continued for a while in the Leicester area, with a guard taking the fares, just like a bus. What ignominy for proud railwaymen. Everything finished completely in May 1969. The track was finally taken up, the demolition squads moved in, anything worth saving was dragged to the knackers' yards. A main-line life had ended. Railway Ramblers were soon to begin ...

3 York

WHAT A SCHOOL HAS DONE TO
A STATION AND A LOOK AT THE WORLD'S
GREATEST RAILWAY MUSEUM

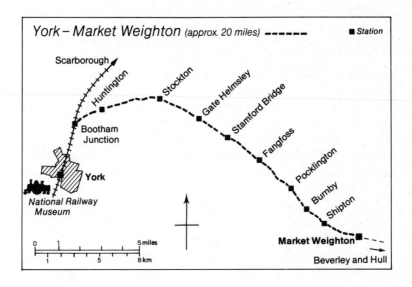

York – Market Weighton (approx. 20 miles) - - - - - - ■ Station

Scarborough

Huntington

Stockton

Gate Helmsley

Stamford Bridge

Fangfoss

Pocklington

Burnby

Shipton

Bootham Junction

York

National Railway Museum

Market Weighton

Beverley and Hull

0   1   5 miles
1   5   8 km

WHEN YOU THINK how the country has been shorn of living railway lines these last two decades, one wonders how York has managed to escape so lightly. Only one line into the city has been closed and the railway map of York and district looks much the same today, with almost every vein still in black, as it did at the beginning of the century.

Today's Inter-City, Inter-Galactic, Advanced Passenger, Terribly Secret, Heavily Experimental, all seem to take in York as they hurtle up from London to Edinburgh. Yet if you had a look at the map of eastern Britain, with a clear and unprejudiced eye, you would see that the quickest way between the two capitals is via Leeds, keeping well to the left of little old York, pretty though it may be. The A1 main road keeps well away from York as it goes North, and always did, even in its stage-coach days. The modern M1 peters out at Leeds, not York. I'm surprised at Dr Beeching. What has York got that put it on the railway map and has kept it there?

The answer is railway history. Mr George Hudson, the first and greatest of the Railway Kings, came from York and he made it his business to see that York was never bypassed. When the railway companies started throwing their lines all over the place, he made sure York was on their map. Once York became established as a vital link on the eastern run, it was very hard to budge. Today, it is still the regional headquarters for British Railways.

At one time seven different companies ran into York, a record equalled by Carlisle, and its historic railway buildings and connections have always been well loved by railway fans. But since 1975 there's been a new development which has put York on the national, even the world map, as a centre for railway enthusiasts. York's railway life looks assured for centuries to come.

I set off for York, therefore like a pilgrim, full of excitement and awe, hardly able to believe that the shrine could stand up to all my expectations. The Inter-City 125 wonder from King's Cross was a bit of a let-down. The water boiler had gone on the blink and the buffet was unable to provide tea or coffee, though they kept up an incessant stream of apologies on their smart intercom all the way, which helped to pass the time, especially as the accents of the apologists moved from Scottish to West Indian, from Cockney to Geordie.

York railway station is greatly loved by all railway fans, combining some of the best features of Victorian railway architecture with a chance to see the latest railway hardware and devices which are frequently being tried out in York. It was opened in 1877 (replacing an older station) and was proclaimed at the time as the largest station in the world. It is now a Grade 1 listed building and has recently been renovated, the yellow brickwork sandblasted and the NER wrought-iron heraldic shields repainted in the correct colours.

In 1942, platforms 1, 2 and 3 were damaged by German bombs, during a night raid on the city. The King's Cross–Edinburgh sleeper, which was standing on platform 9, was also destroyed, but some brave work by station staff saved all the passengers.

As in all old stations, you have to let your eyes wander slowly round, gently taking in the decorations which most people miss as they hurry to get out, rarely looking up and around them. The curved roof is a wonder in itself, over 800 feet long and 234 feet wide, but perhaps the most attractive and best preserved parts are platforms 4–7, at the northern end of the station, which have been used as the setting for many TV and feature films, such as Warner Brothers' *Agatha* and the BBC's *Race to the North*.

The days of top-hatted, frock-coated railway staff are gone – most senior staff had to wear top-hats at some time – but the area manager, who has a local staff of 1,200 under his control, often puts on his bowler for formal occasions. As York contains the HQ for Eastern Region, another historic Victorian building, also recently cleaned up, they do get many VIPs.

However, I couldn't spend too long in York station as I wanted to get going on my disused line, so I took a taxi to the small market town of Pocklington, some fourteen miles along part of the old York–Hull line, determined to walk along it and back into the city. That was the plan, anyway.

This line, one of the original branch lines which formed the North Eastern Railway, dates back to 1847 and became the direct line between York and Hull, via Market Weighton and Beverley. In the 1960s, BR decided to single thirty-one miles of double track from York to Beverley, in order to save money as traffic had decreased. They also planned to install automatic controlled barriers at nineteen level crossings. In 1965, by which time some of this expensive new work had begun, BR decided to call it a day and closed the line. There is now no direct link from York to Hull.

'Land associated with this railway has been disposed of privately in a piecemeal fashion,' replied the planning officer in York when I wrote and asked what had happened to the line.

In 1966 a gentleman called Guy Willatt, well known in the 1950s as a cricketer when he played for Derbyshire, came for an interview to be headmaster of Pocklington School. He happened to notice, as he went into the school, that there was an old station right opposite the school. It looked derelict, as far as he could see, but he thought to himself, what on earth can I do with that, if I get the job?

He got the job, and steered the school through various educational upheavals, such as changing from Direct Grant to Independent, and he also managed to look into the future of the disused station. With a bit of persuading, he eventually talked the Governors into buying it. He would appear to have got a bargain as the school bought the station, the stationmaster's house and four railway cottages for only £6,600.

The little station had already been listed, its architectural worth was known, but the front had been boarded up. When the boarding was removed, five very handsome brick arches were revealed. Perhaps the most surprising thing about the station, which served only the local community with a population of never more than 5,000, was its size. The North Eastern was very aware of its exalted position, as can be shown in the grandeur of York station, and it built to impress the world, and itself.

At Pocklington, they built a large roof over the double track, from side to side, in iron work and glass, open at either end, covering a length of some 66 yards. It must have cost a fortune, even in the 1860s, and seems rather pointless. Why keep the trains covered for the few minutes they were in Pocklington station? Did they not want the station-master to get the wind in his eyes, or any rain on his top hat, when he gazed out of the impressive bow window of his office and watched the trains go by?

It was covered in weeds and the windows and doors were all broken when Mr Willatt took it over, but he knew exactly what he wanted to do with it, though it took three years of delays, what with the purchase and the various planning permissions.

First of all, the platforms either side were removed and a new floor was laid across on wooden blocks. Each end of the station was bricked up and heating and lighting were installed. Lo and behold, Pocklington School had acquired one of the most impressive indoor sports complexes owned by any school in the country, private or state.

Mr Willatt took me into the sports hall and at one end I watched three practice cricket sessions in progress, using full-sized nets. At the other end, which is divided off by a curtain, easily parted when the whole lot is used as one, an indoor football game was taking place. The hall also has markings to turn it into two badminton courts, three basketball courts, or a tennis court. To give you some idea of the total size, when they use it for the school speech day they can accommodate 1,500 people sitting down.

At the first speech day in their new sports hall, Mr Willatt happened to say that the only problem they'd found so far was that when a ball hit the walls the old red brick, now over a hundred years old, tended to raise a slight dust. In the audience was a vice-chairman of ICI, one of the parents, who said he would send some of his chemists to solve the problem. 'They sprayed it with something. I don't know what. But the problem immediately disappeared.'

Mr Willatt has since addressed national teaching bodies on the conversion of his old station, and has had many letters from institutions thinking of doing the same. There are, at this moment, several thousand old stations in the country which no one is sure how to use. He was lucky, of course, in having such a spacious station, with its roof in very good condition, right on his doorstep, but he saw the possibilities when others hadn't. One of his own rules is never to build new when you can convert.

The Sports Council gave the school a grant of £20,000, and for this they have to open the station for local use, five nights a week. The total cost of conversion, including the £20,000 grant, came to £55,000. Mr Willatt was told when the work was finished that a sports hall of a similar size would have cost £180,000. Today, it would be nearer half a million.

'We don't just have a perfect sports hall, we have an *attractive* one. The normal sports hall is concrete and clinical, white and impersonal. This beautiful old brick makes it warm and welcoming.'

They've retained the long, arched windows and of course the deep red brickwork. The original station lavatories have been extended and used as changing rooms. The station-master's house, which was part of the station itself, is now the PE master's house. He can look out of the lovely box window, not in his top hat but in his track suit, watching the boys at play.

I took so long admiring the conversion, and examining all the railway relics which the headmaster has put in the changing rooms and table-tennis rooms, such as real railway platform seats, notices and old posters, that when he offered me a lift into York, I accepted.

I was supposed to be walking into York. I was supposed to be looking at the rest of the disused railway line, from Pocklington into York. This is supposed to be a book about *walking* old tracks. Well, perhaps I'll do it another time. I have to admit that unfortunately I didn't walk the old line into York. As I'd made a date in York with another Important Railway Person, I couldn't be late. So, I graciously accepted a lift from one of the sixth formers, using the headmaster's Volvo.

My driver, sixth former Richard Bradley, a farmer's son from Wensleydale, told me he'd probably spent more time in the sports hall than in any other part of the school in his ten years there. The school today has 700 boys, half of them boarders, plus 17 day girls. It was founded in 1514 and is one of the oldest schools in Yorkshire. William Wilberforce went there. He wrote his first anti-slavery letter to the Press while still a pupil.

Richard thought it a shame, in one way, that the railway had gone, as for generations it had been very handy for the school. His father before him had been at Pocklington and had good memories of the station in active use. 'He always tells me about the time he and some friends borrowed bikes from the kitchen staff one evening and went out of bounds into Beverley to see some girls. They came back on the train, with their bikes, and meant to get off at the station before Pock, knowing they might be seen, but they missed the stop and had to get off at Pock. They crept off the train, with their bikes, straight into the arms of the head. They all got six of the best.'

In York, I still had a few minutes to spare, so I went looking for Hudson Street, a recycled name for a very old street. As a plaque at the end states, it had originally been called Hudson Street, but in 1849 when George Hudson 'fell from grace' it was changed to Railway Street. In 1971, it reverted back to Hudson Street. The plaque is on the wall of a brightly painted hotel, the Railway King, which also suffered a transmogrification in 1971, dropping its old name of Adelphi and becoming the Railway King, in honour again of George Hudson.

Visitors to York, unacquainted with railway history, must find all these changes rather confusing. There's no clue to the identity of Mr Hudson or why he 'fell from grace'.

I walked into the pub, hoping for further information, and came to a door on the left marked George Hudson Bar. A notice pinned to it said, 'Sorry NO SOLDIERS allowed in this bar'. That didn't help, except to confuse me further. Where are all the soldiers in York?

George Hudson was born in 1800 in a village outside York, the son of a yeoman farmer. He left home at fifteen to work in York as an assistant on the counter in a linen draper's shop. He did well enough in the shop, becoming a partner, though this was partly through marrying one of the partners' daughters, a lady five years his senior. He had some even better luck when he was twenty-seven, rushing to the bedside of a remote relation, a great-uncle, who was dying. George was the only person present when the relation died, leaving a will in which George

got everything, a small fortune of £30,000, to everyone's surprise, and a few people's suspicions.

Overnight, he turned himself into one of York's thrusting
businessmen, moving into the right political, social and financial
circles. In 1833 there was talk of the railway coming to York
and George became one of the local promoters. The following
year he met George Stephenson who fired his imagination with
talk of covering the whole country with a network of railways.
Using his friendship with Stephenson to drum up financial
support and get the right bill through Parliament, he eventually
created the York and North Midlands Railways in 1836 – which
in turn became the North Eastern.

Hudson quickly expanded his empire, taking over other companies, creating new ones, and the grateful citizens of York,
recognising that he'd put York on the railway map of Britain,
elected him Lord Mayor. His reign as Lord Mayor was noted
for his lavishness, with enormous banquets for his hangers-on
and backers, paid for by council funds.

In ten years from opening his first railway, Hudson had built
up from scratch a railway empire worth £30 million. He became
the toast of London, feted by the aristocracy, introduced to
royalty, a friend and adviser to the Duke of Wellington. The
whole country was of course railway mad during the 1840s and
enormous profits were being made by the railway companies.
People fought to buy shares in any scheme Hudson mentioned,
even when he gave no details. The financing of railway companies was a new science and George, as its first and greatest
exponent, made up his own rules as he went along, juggling the
books to suit his own purpose. As one wit of the time noted,
Hudson kept everything, except his own accounts.

One of his early master strokes took place up in Yorkshire
when a rival railway company, the Manchester and Leeds,
dared to put forward a scheme for a branch line from York to
Hull, via Market Weighton. One of the many problems which
every railway company had was in buying up the necessary
land, or in some way doing a deal with the local landowners.
When you look at strange loops on an old railway map the
reason is very often because some long-forgotten deal fell
through.

Hudson looked at the map and realised that his rival's line would go through land belonging to the Duke of Devonshire. Hudson moved in first – and bought the lot! For half a million pounds, he got the Londesborough Park and 12,000 acres. This was in 1845, but even then the cost of his deal amazed the nation. His supporters were entranced and his rivals greatly alarmed. He moved with his wife into the Duke's stately home and in 1847 opened his own York to Market Weighton line, building himself his own private railway station, planting a magnificent avenue of trees, two miles long, down which he could be driven from his own house. In the process, he sold a little bit of his estate, to his own company, for a profit of £18,000. Nice one, George.

This is the line, through Pocklington, which I had intended to walk. Now I remember why I thought is was so important. I am told his private station at Londesborough has gone, but the avenue of trees is still there. Some day I'll go and look for them.

Hudson's fall began not long afterwards. By 1849 his rivals had known for some time that he was cooking the books, but no one could ever prove it. As long as railways were expanding, and money was pouring in, George always kept ahead. His method was very simple. Every time he had to pay out investors, he opened a new company. Old debts could therefore be paid with the rush of new money, a system which was later made illegal. To keep his supporters happy – and his friends and associates made millions out of his schemes – he often paid dividends *before* a railway had opened, when there was still no income.

Eventually saturation point was reached and several companies did go bankrupt, as there were just too many railways chasing too little money. Two London stockbrokers, who personally lost money in a company run by Hudson, decided to go up to York and expose his methods. After a great deal of exhaustive research, they managed to nail him at a railway company meeting in York. He was eventually forced to admit, amongst many misdemeanours that yes, he had added a nought on the company accounts. In fact, he might have added a few noughts. He couldn't quite remember.

Other railway companies up and down the country in which

he was involved did similar investigations and very soon his whole empire was collapsing. In one company's accounts, under the heading 'Secret Service', it was revealed that he had spent hundreds of thousands of pounds bribing MPs to get his railway bills through Parliament.

The rise had been quick, but the fall was dramatic. All the guilt and corruption and obscenely bloated profits which characterised that decade of railway madness turned into a Victorian witch-hunt, directed personally at Hudson. His brother-in-law, who had been a front man in many deals, committed suicide. Hudson at least did the decent thing, fleeing to France where he lived like a pauper for the next twenty years, without ever naming names or bringing down any of the famous and powerful people for whom he had made fortunes. In York, they immediately erased his name from the Aldermanic record books and hurriedly changed Hudson Street to Railway Street.

It was in 1971, exactly a hundred years after his death, that his name reappeared on the streets of York. There had been no sudden revelations that he had been a goody after all; just a slow realisation that, on the centenary of his death, one need not look on all the bad things. He had after all created some excellent railways, such as the North Eastern, and he had started the process of amalgamation which proceeded long after his death, ending with the big four in 1923: the LNER (which came out of Hudson's empire), the LMS (which also included part of his old empire), the GWR and the Southern. Most of all, it was Hudson who had first put York on the railway map.

I walked from Hudson Street through York to the National Railway Museum, living proof of York's fame as a railway centre. The new museum is in Leeman Road, named after the York solicitor who was one of those instrumental in bringing about Hudson's downfall.

The country's first ever railway museum was set up in York by the London and North Eastern Railway in 1927. The new national one, which has a completely refurbished building, was opened in 1975. British Railways passed on to them their collection from Clapham, York and elsewhere, and provided a substantial site and building, right beside the main-line station, then they took no further direct interest.

The new museum is a branch of the Science Museum and is the most marvellous, lovingly cared for, warm and glowing, colourful and exciting museum I've ever been to. The figures speak for themselves. It was expected to attract 500,000 visitors a year, which was the brief the architect was given. Instead they've been getting $1\frac{1}{2}$ million a year, and have had to hurriedly expand the lavatories, shops and other facilities accordingly. In an age of Civil Service cuts, they've managed to increase their staff, if only just, from 75 to 76. It now has the biggest attendance of any museum anywhere outside London. Over seven million visitors have lovingly patted the buffers, so they have now been lacquered. You can touch everything, and all Railway Romantics love touching, being sensual beasts at heart.

There's one amazing locomotive, which has had its insides opened up like a dissected whale, with all the different elements painted. You press one of forty-five buttons, from Tender to Mechanical Lubrication, and the appropriate part lights up. Seven million pairs of sweaty little hands have deposited a lot of human grease on these buttons, at one time fouling up the electrical contacts, but they are regularly checked.

Considering the enormous crowds, everything is in terrific condition, with every locomotive gleaming and bright as a new painting. In fact on my first sight of all the treasures, looking down from the balcony, I had a feeling that despite the fearful size of all the monsters, I was really looking at the colourful pages of one of the Rev. Audrey's little books about Henry and James and the other toy engines. The museum covers two acres and the preserved engines and carriages of which around fifty are on show at any one time, are grouped round two turntables. If you stand in the middle of one of the circles, you can imagine they are all steaming towards you, about to run you down, which of course is how any true railway fan would like to go.

The two most popular exhibits are *Mallard*, the beautiful blue locomotive which broke the world speed record for steam in 1938 with 126 miles per hour, and Queen Victoria's royal saloon of 1869, a riot of vulgar colours and obscenely luxurious soft furnishings. Third most popular exhibit, so Dr John Coiley, the Museum's Keeper, says is the Advanced Passenger Train. This pleases him highly. 'Railways are very much alive and I consider part of our duty is to show the future of railways, not just look back.'

He gets upset if people think it's just a steam museum, as they devote a great deal of time and space to electrical and diesel engineering and have examples and explanations on most of the modern developments, such as computerised control of railway systems.

'There are many exciting things happening in British industry today, look at Concorde, body scanners, North Sea oil rigs. Where, for example, could an ordinary school boy of today see an actual space capsule until one was put in the Science Museum in London? We're still a leading technological country and I feel it's a duty of modern museums to show things like that, things we're still jolly good at. That's why we try to tell a modern story here, as well as a past one.'

The museum also has an academic purpose. There are many rather esoteric types of exhibits, apart from all the glamorous old locos, such as displays which show the history of signalling or railway tickets. They have an excellent collection of railway books, documents, maps and parliamentary bills, which are available to scholars.

They get a great many foreign visitors, although they don't cover foreign railways in the museum, unless there's a strong British connection. British connections are, in fact, almost everywhere in the world. From the Stephensons onwards, British engineers were in great demand in Europe, Asia and North America. The first railways in Belgium, Holland and Germany all used British-built locomotives.

As a generalisation, their foreign visitors tend to be North Europeans, from Germany and Holland. The Mediterraneans, judging by the lack of Spanish, Italian and to some extent French visitors, don't seem so interested in railways. It has often been suggested that there is a form of sexual sublimation in a passion for old steam engines. Perhaps the Latins prefer the real thing.

There are some excellent railway museums abroad. The French have a good one at Mulhouse, near the German border. They deliberately put it there, knowing they would get lots of

German enthusiasts coming over to visit it. Yet France has the world's biggest railway magazine, *La Vie du Rail*, which sells 280,000 copies a week. It even has the TV programmes and women's pages.

The Germans, who only quite recently gave up steam on their public lines, have their museum at Nuremberg. The Indians have one in Delhi and in the USA there's a good one growing up at Sacramento, while the Smithsonian in Washington has some good national railway relics.

Dr Coiley and Peter Semmens, York's Assistant Keeper, have between them been to most of these museums, and in turn had official visitors back. They both agreed, with due modesty when pressed, that York was probably the best, the biggest, the most popular of them all.

We all went for a walk together round the museum. Mr Semmens pointed out a little cabinet showing railway advertising, how old railway companies had their own house styles, distinctive logos and markings, a feature we tend to associate with modern multinational companies. He showed me a pack of cards produced by the Great Central, the line I walked at Leicester, the sort of gifts which later became popular with airlines. There was a very nice LNER fan, complete with insignia, which at one time was given out to first-class lady passengers.

I pressed my nose up close to the pre-war royal carriages, admiring all the royal furniture, the scrambler telephone to hand, the desk open, the royal headed notepaper waiting for the royal pen. Mr Semmens said I could go inside, though it's not normally open, but I declined, feeling it might be an intrusion. The royal family deserve some privacy, even *in absentia*.

Despite Dr Coiley's aim to make it a museum of the present as well as the past, it was obvious they haven't lost their own love of old railways. I asked each for his personal favourite thing in the whole museum; one object they would like to take home. Both chose old locos. Dr Coiley said his favourite was *Evening Star*, the last steam locomotive to be built by British Rail. He had a personal interest because as a young man he saw it being built at Swindon in 1960.

Peter Semmens chose *Gladstone*, a much older engine, built in 1882 for the London, Brighton and South Coast Railway. It doesn't look all that powerful or dramatic, compared with some of the mighty engines nearby, but it would probably be in every enthusiast's top three in a railway Miss World contest. It is so pretty you can hardly believe it's real. It's a lush browny, chocolate colour and usually has a royal coat of arms at the front, the regalia formerly carried by L.B. and S.C.R.'s royal trains. However, he chose it for personal and historic reasons, as well as its sheer beauty. *Gladstone* was the first locomotive to be preserved by a railway society when in 1927 it was obtained from the Southern Railway by the Stephenson Locomotive Society. (Mr Semmens is a past chairman of that society.) It went on display at the original railway museum in York and became one of the founding exhibits of today's National Collection. It's now a museum piece, in every sense.

Every true enthusiast who goes to York drools about *Gladstone*. But you don't need to be a railway fan to visit York. Anyone interested in the history of Britain, and its future, shouldn't miss the National Railway Museum.

Because of the enormous crowds, it's best to keep your visit for the winter months, from October to March. If it has to be the summer, try a Friday or a Saturday. A lot of visitors to York travel on those days, either starting or ending their holidays.

Cup Final day is a perfect day to go. Usually on a Spring Saturday they get 8,000 visitors but every Cup Final day since they opened, the number has dropped dramatically to 3,000, regardless of which teams are in the Final.

The time to avoid, at any season, is a Sunday afternoon. That might well be the best time to talk to the headmaster of Pocklington School into letting you see his old station, or perhaps to go for a walk down the old track to look for George Hudson's trees.

4 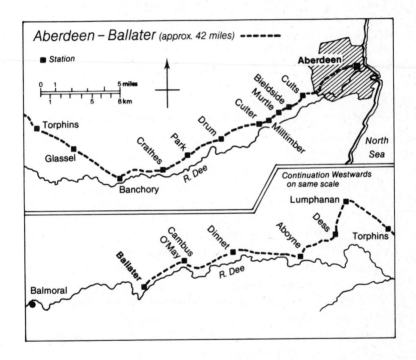 The Deeside Line

From Aberdeen to Ballater
with some Royal Trains and
some Royal Connections

Aberdeen – Ballater (approx. 42 miles)

■ Station

0 1 5 miles
1 5 8 km

Aberdeen

Cults
Bieldside
Murtle
Culter
Milltimber
Drum
Park
Crathes
R. Dee
Banchory
Glassel
Torphins

North Sea

Continuation Westwards on same scale

Lumphanan
Dess
Aboyne
Torphins
Dinnet
Cambus O'May
Ballater
R. Dee
Balmoral

TRAINS AND ROYALTY arrived on Deeside around the same time, which was fortunate for all concerned. Deeside to this day proudly calls itself Royal Deeside and is deservedly famous as one of Scotland's finest tourist attractions. Royalty did itself a huge favour when it bought Balmoral, still the only real retreat that the royal family has.

It was in the late 1840s, at the height of Britain's Railway Mania, that a line was first proposed up the river Dee from Aberdeen. There was already a road along the north bank of the Dee, from the timber mills down to Aberdeen. There were the usual sort of objections from the local landed gentry at the very idea of a railway. In this case it was the Duke of Cleveland who forbade his tenantry to permit surveys for the Deeside Railways on any parts of his estate, 'nor are they to give refreshments or shelter, even in a barn, to any of the employees'. The original plans fell through but were later resurrected on a slightly different route, and the first railway service, between Aberdeen and Banchory, opened in 1853.

It was also in the late 1840s that Queen Victoria and Dear Albert started having holidays on Deeside, leasing property at Balmoral. In 1851, the *Aberdeen Journal* stated proudly that they were 'happy to announce that the beautiful estate of Balmoral, in this county, the Highland home of our beloved Sovereign for about four years past is now "Royal Property"'. Albert had bought the land outright and given it as a gift to the Queen.

The Queen first travelled on the Deeside line in October 1853, after her mother, the Duchess of Kent, had tested it out two days previously and expressed herself 'highly pleased with all the arrangements'. The Queen herself was late for her first trip on the Deeside line, being delayed on her twenty-four-mile coach ride from Balmoral to Banchory by heavy rains which flooded the road, but once on the train to Aberdeen everything went smoothly and all along the line 'crowds of lieges were assembled and testified their loyalty in hearty manner'.

Throughout the nineteenth century and up until the First World War, there were rapturous crowds throughout Britain whenever a royal train was expected. Londoners had always been accustomed to royal processions, but with the arrival of trains, remote country areas, if they happened to have a railway patronised by royalty, were given their own little state occasions, often with great pomp and pageantry, as the rival railway companies competed to make their royal coaches even more splendid and ornate.

Queen Victoria's very first railway ride, on any train, took place on 13 June 1842 and was an important day in the history of trains. It set the seal on railways, which were still being attacked in many quarters as being dangerous, unreliable, not fit for gentlefolk, nasty and dirty, liable to make pheasants flee and cows to miscarry, and probably only a passing fad anyway.

The Great Western Railway had been hoping since 1840 that the Queen would one day use the train to return from Windsor Castle to London, thereby using their line. They'd even built a special royal carriage, designed by a famous London coach-builder and upholstered in Bond Street with hanging sofas in the style of Louis xv, panelled walls, rich silks and fine paintings. For two years, they'd had this magnificent royal carriage all ready and waiting, till in June 1842 the royal summons finally came.

The Queen was shown over the train on her arrival at Slough, where the directors of the GWR turned out to greet her. The engine, *Phlegethon*, was driven to London by its designer Daniel Gooch, the GWR's Locomotive Superintendent, and he was accompanied on the engine by Isambard Kingdom Brunel, the GWR's Engineer – two of the greatest figures in locomotive history, household names in all railway households.

Her Majesty was very pleased with the experience and wrote to her Uncle Leopold, King of the Belgians, that it had been agreeably free from the dust and the noise of travel by road. The romance of stage-coach travel has led us to believe that coaches were somehow cleaner and nicer than smoky railways, forgetting of course how dangerous coach travel was, with numerous accidents, endless noise in crowded cobbled streets and either dust or mud everywhere, depending on the weather.

It wasn't just in luxury fittings, fit for a queen, that the railway companies competed with each other. They also put in the latest technical developments and inventions, many of which later became standard for all passengers. The next year, 1843, the Queen graced a special royal carriage provided by the London and Birmingham Railway which included a hot-water heater, fed by a small boiler under the floor – the first railway carriage in history to have any sort of heating.

In 1850, the GWR built a new Queen's Carriage which had the first ever train lavatory. It was probably Prince Albert's suggestion, as he'd recently been adding similar modern refinements in the royal palaces.

Queen Victoria's first long train ride was in 1848 when she came south from her summer holiday at Balmoral. This was before the Deeside line had been built, so the royal party was forced to go by coach to Montrose, then the northern railhead. It was a last-minute decision as the royal yacht, which had been meant to take them home, was caught in bad weather. The Queen made the entire journey south in an ordinary first-class compartment, doing it in three stages, with overnight stops at Perth and Crewe.

Throughout her reign, her annual trip to Balmoral was normally by train, there and back, usually taking 18 hours over each journey. One timetable for 1895 shows her leaving Windsor at 8.20 on the evening of Tuesday 21 May and arriving at Ballater at 2.35 the next afternoon. The party slept on the train overnight and usually got out at Perth in the morning for an hour to have breakfast with the local railway directors.

The Great Western took her on the first stage, from Windsor to Wolverhampton; the London and North Western took her on through Wigan to Carlisle; the Caledonian then took over to Perth and Aberdeen. In Aberdeen, with a little bit of shunting and reversing, she finally left the main line and was transferred to the branch line, the Royal Deeside line to Ballater.

There were no corridors on the early trains, not even in the royal compartments, so when she wanted a different lady-in-waiting to join her, she had to wait for the next station. This often happened at Beattock, on the long haul up and over the Scottish Border hills. As there was no proper platform at Beattock, ladies-in-waiting often had to be helped up into the royal coach, with a bit of undignified pushing from below.

John Brown, the Queen's famous Highland servant, was usually on the Balmoral run. He had his little accommodation area at the end of the Queen's night-time saloon and didn't need to jump coaches if required for any services during the journey.

The London and North Western was the first to put in gas lighting in its royal coach. And the Queen insisted on its immediate removal. She much preferred oil or candles and throughout her life demanded oil lamps in all her coaches. This naturally worried the railway designers, concerned about spillages and the risk of fire when a train was travelling at speed, but the Queen was also against speed, so that lessened the risk. She insisted on never travelling at more than 40 miles per hour, which was one reason why it took her so long to reach Balmoral.

She was also terribly conservative about meals on trains, and refused them throughout her long reign, even though dining cars had been in use since 1879. Instead, everyone in her party had to have a good tea before leaving on the evening train, and to tighten their belts till they could tuck into a big breakfast at Perth.

Even in 1897, at the time of her Diamond Jubilee, when the GWR produced a complete new royal train, with all the latest luxuries, she insisted on retaining her old royal carriage, now twenty-three years old, for her personal use. She'd discovered that they'd put electricity throughout the new royal coaches, and was horrified. She still preferred to have the immense cloche-shaped oil lamp hanging from the domed ceiling of her old carriage.

Bathrooms were first introduced on royal trains in 1914, with silver-plated taps and panelled casings, one of the improvements first put in for royalty that hasn't filtered down to become standard use. During the First World War, George v and Queen Mary lived in their royal train for many days at a time, touring the munitions factories, and so a bathroom was as much a necessity as a luxury.

Perhaps the most exotic and luxurious of all royal trains were those provided by a small company, the London, Tilbury and

Southend, who had the honour of transporting Edward VII and George V during their coronation celebrations. The engine on each occasion was garlanded with patriotic flags, and arms and busts of the King and Queen were mounted at the front of the engine, just above the buffer. Between the heads, there was a little fountain, using water supplied from the locomotive's tanks. All the caps and cases and outward fittings of the engine were specially plated in nickel.

It was all part of the nineteenth-century passion for turning royal train rides into state occasions, a passion which ended with the horrors of the First World War when such needless expenditure was thought unseemly. Today's royal family still travel in specially made royal carriages, constructed for their own private use, and their progress is suitably regal, but in a more dignified, less ostentatious manner. The days of a royal train ride being a little coronation are over.

You can still see some of these royal coaches at York and of course any visitor to the Royal Deeside line, the most famous royal route, is overwhelmed by images of what these royal occasions must have been like.

The Great North of Scotland Railway took over the running of the line from the original Deeside Railway Company in 1866, the year in which it was extended to Ballater, its final stopping place, some forty-two miles from Aberdeen and about six from Balmoral.

In 1923 the Great North of Scotland became part of the LNER and in turn was inherited by BR on nationalisation in 1948. The line finally closed in 1966 to some considerable local weeping and wailing, though not enough to save it, one of those little branch lines which fell quickly to Dr Beeching's axe, despite all its royal history and its supporters maintaining that the losses were due to bad railway management rather than lack of passengers.

Now that the tourist trade is more important than ever to this part of Scotland, as well as to Britain as a whole, and the price of petrol so high, it does seem a shame that the line could not have had a longer lease of life. There can be few valleys anywhere in Britain with such a wealth of historical, literary, royal, natural and industrial associations. I found it the richest, in every way, of all my railway walks. I could have spent a year exploring it, not just the few spring days I was lucky enough to manage.

The first eight miles are today a splendid public walkway, run by the City of Aberdeen, and the final eight or so miles to Ballater are also in public ownership, though not as yet converted. In between, private landowners and developers have to a greater or lesser extent roped off several stretches, but in the main the line has been left to grow wild. It means that the majority of the line can be freely walked, either with judicious trespassing or by using the nearby road, which in the non-tourist season is a pleasant walk in itself.

The eight-mile Aberdeen conversion which has taken place was seen as a prototype for all such plans in the rest of Scotland, though most of them have not yet taken place, owing to lack of money or lack of courage and foresight. The Countryside Commission for Scotland produced a report in 1971 on the then completely disused Deeside line. The Commission was very worried that such a valuable national asset was going to waste, and pointed out that there were already 1,683 miles of closed lines in Scotland, compared with just 1,930 miles still in operation.

Aberdeen University helped by producing a fascinating survey, done by their Department of Botany, which did an intensive investigation of two short stretches of the line, at either end, in 1973. This is still a blueprint for all local bodies interested in the potential of their local disused railways; final proof, if it were still needed, of the unique natural resources on every old railway line. In one two-and-a-half-acre stretch, only four miles or so from the very centre of Aberdeen, between Cults and Peterculter, still a heavily suburban area, which had been well walked and well used since the closure, they found 150 different plant species. 'Most striking', so they remarked in their report. (The East Grinstead figures were higher, but that was over a longer sample and in open countryside.)

As the report points out, with the increasing passion of farmers for cutting down hedges, replacing them with fences, we are not only losing rich tree and plant life, but all the animals and insects that live and thrive in such hedges. On an old railway, however, where nettles and thistles are usually allowed to grow freely, you now get more butterflies than anywhere else in the country. Butterflies love nettles and thistles, and the rotting fruit on wild bramble and raspberry bushes. The report named a total of ten different butterflies they had spotted – common blue, large white, green veined white, small copper, red admiral, meadow brown, small white, small tortoiseshell, grayling, painted lady.

As for the 150 different forms of plant life, they are too numerous to mention – but they range from short-lived plants like sticky groundsel and ivy-leaved toadflax to trees like syca-more, ash, beech, cherry, elm, scrub birch and willow. They also noticed garden escapees such as solomon's seal and budd-leia. In addition, they found thirty different forms of mosses and lichens, often growing on the damp walls of old station buildings.

The section at the other end of the line, deep in wild Highland countryside, with a different topography and climate, was even richer. Taken together, the two little railway patches, some thirty miles apart, produced a total of 249 different plants. Just to finish off the figures, they also identified twenty-eight differ-ent birds on the two stretches – blackbird, house sparrow, greenfinch, willow warbler, partridge, wood pigeon, black-headed gull, lesser redpoll, great tit, missel thrush, starling, yellow hammer, whitethroat, song thrush, blackcap, crow, wren, blue tit, pheasant, herring gull, swallow, house martin, oyster-catcher, chaffinch, dunnock, goldcrest, rook, robin.

Suitably loaded with fascinating facts, I started off my walk from Aberdeen, looking for royal connections as well as flora and fauna, though I was far from confident of my ability to spot a dunnock from a lesser redpoll. I would have to take the experts' words for that.

The little booklet on The Old Deeside Line Walk, produced by the City of Aberdeen's Leisure Department, which has a map of their eight-mile conversion, shows the walk beginning beside Duthie Park, in the Ruthrieston district of the city, not far from the George VI bridge over the river Dee. It was nice to start with a royal connection.

I greatly admired the hosts and hosts of golden daffodils which were in full bloom all along the banks of the Dee, between the George VI bridge and the Bridge of Dee. It must cost the council quite a lot to maintain, but then Aberdeen is today the boom city of Scotland, if not the whole of Britain, now that it's the centre for the North Sea oil trade. All that day I looked for railway walkers wearing stetsons and cowboy boots, as the rest of Britain has been led to believe that the whole of Aberdeen has been overrun with Yanks. I didn't see one.

The cost of converting the line, back in 1972, was put at £1,000 a mile, which seems to me a bargain. The main job was to replace the heavy railway ballast, which all railway ramblers know to their cost makes for awkward walking, with a finer, light-coloured gravel, and to seed the edges where necessary. Maintenance costs were equally modest, estimated at between £150 and £250 a mile. Maintenance must have gone up appreciably since then, but as the council don't have any wardening staff, unlike some converted lines, it still can't be too expensive.

I had asked in the hotel I was staying at, the Tulloch Lodge in Ballater, at the other end of the line, if anyone had ever walked it, but neither of the two proprietors had done so. One said he didn't like the look of it.

I have to admit that my first glimpse of the track, when I eventually found it, did make it seem rather urban and concrete-like. The new surface looks almost white from a distance and though it provides a perfect, smooth surface for cyclists, it does give it the appearance of a public park. Real railway ramblers like a bit of wildness about their walks. But after all, this end is right in the heart of an industrial city, with roads and council estates all around. It probably pays the council to keep it park-like and tidy. Once you let things go wild inside a town, then you encourage others to do the same and it becomes a dumping ground.

I expected some plaque or notice, saying 'walkers start here', perhaps even some information about the history of the line, which would be of interest to all visitors, and to the younger generation of natives who must be unaware that it was once a royal railway line. But there was nothing. You just climb up onto it from Polmuir road, with no directions of any sort, and away you go along the path.

I admired to my left the fine greenhouses in Duthie Park, a gift from Miss Duthie of Ruthrieston to the citizens of Aberdeen and opened by Princess Beatrice in 1883. More royal connections. The park is now one of the most popular open spaces in the city with boating and model yachting. Inside the greenhouses, so I was told, there are exotic palms. With so much to look at on the line ahead, I was determined not to be seduced down culs-de-sac, however enticing.

A gang of boys on bikes watched my progress with interest, but not hostility. They kept tearing past me, back and forth, along the first few miles. I didn't see anyone else walking the line, for the pleasure of the walk itself, even though it was the Easter holidays. Perhaps in the height of the summer they get more walkers, though with the lack of signposts, outsiders will find it hard to discover the line.

I stopped to talk to a lady who was painting the fence at the bottom of her garden. She said she's lived beside the line for forty years and had happy memories of rushing to her windows when the young princesses, Elizabeth and Margaret, were going past. The path is so narrow here and the buildings so close, that it must have been possible to gape right into the faces of the royal family, without even leaving your own house.

'Most of the time they kept their curtains closed,' she added. 'Well, they deserved their privacy. They get even less privacy today. I feel sorry for them. That's why they love Balmoral, the only place they can really get away from everyone.'

She didn't mind too much that the railway had closed, especially now it had been converted so neatly by the council. 'It means people keep their dogs off the streets.' She blamed the royal family as much as the ordinary passengers for its demise. 'They didn't support it either in the last years. They started flying to Dyce airport and then going on by car to Balmoral.'

The first bridge I walked over was marked 1002, as a guide for railway workers and engine-drivers. The second, number 1003, has been pulled down, at least its middle has gone so you can't get across. I had to go down some steps into the main road, past David Duncan, Surgical Bootmaker, and then up the other side, back on to the track again. It looked as if at one time there had been a little station or a halt on the line round here, judging by the long platform that still remains.

In the first flush of killing off the line, several of the bridges over main roads on the outskirts of the city were taken down, to save their upkeep, which means you have to climb down a couple of times, but it's easy to do so and quite interesting, giving you a low-level view of the area's streets and front doors, instead of being up above, seeing only the gardens and rear views. At bridge 1005 I came to what might have been another little station or halt. Silver birch trees had taken up their positions in the cracks in the concrete.

Walking ahead of me, I could see an elderly couple, each with a shopping bag. I hurried to catch them up, hoping for some memories, but they were turning into a back garden gate, just as I came abreast. They said they used the line every day for bits of shopping in Holburn Street. Verra handy. It meant they never had to walk through the busy streets.

There are various prettifying touches at several spots along the way, such as picnic tables and chairs, but in the main only the track itself has been converted, the sides being left alone. You can't really call them embankments. The whole line of the railway is so narrow and flat and straight that apart from the odd remnants of platforms, you can hardly tell it had once been a railway; it seems just a magical country path which has somehow cut its way in a dead straight line through the suburbs.

A lot of these suburbs came after the railway, and were spawned by it, little granite villas for businessmen in the then green belt, with a handy connection into the bustling city. Today, the commuters, many of them in the oil business, live much further out, right up into Highland Deeside, racing in by car, on the North or South Deeside roads. They are buying up the former holiday homes of Aberdonians, who took their families up the valley for the summer. Time and distance have now been concertina'd and people can accommodate much longer journeys to their place of work.

After 1008, I came to another flourish of daffodils, right alongside the line, the Aberdeen landscaping department having lashed out once again, opening out the railway line to make

[57]

it part of the gardens of a new housing estate. I felt suddenly bare and exposed, open to public view, having so far been in a secret world, creeping through suburbs undetected. I wondered how many people could have given a description of me, seen from their rear windows, if for some reason the police had wanted me.

The burst of parkland pride came to an end when I went under a new-looking concrete bridge, covered with graffiti. Some of it I could easily understand, such as 'Rangers are Wanks' and 'Govan Rule', referring to visiting Glasgow football supporters, but there were three references I couldn't understand – 'This is a Shed Bridge', 'Ya Bas' and 'Mas'. I wondered what they meant. This sort of cryptic communication tends to lose its meaning very quickly, even in its own district.

The first station for many years on the Deeside line, coming from Aberdeen, was Cults, a little village full of merchants' retreats. It's now an extension of Aberdeen's suburbia, but still with a rural air as the river Dee begins to be seen and the fields and mountains beckon ahead. John Duncan, the father of the Deeside Railway, had his impressive little villa, Fuschia Bank, in Cults. The name Cults comes from the Gaelic for wood and at one time it was part of a royal forest, given to Aberdeen in 1319 by King Robert the Bruce.

A boy and a girl, aged about sixteen, were crossing the line and I walked with them for a few hundred yards. The boy pointed out to me that a row of villas near the old station had their front doors facing the line. At one time, the proud owners could come out of their front doors, walk a few yards along the tract to the station, and so on to their train to Aberdeen. Now, with the line abandoned, the villas are facing the wrong way. Their back doors are where the front would normally be, leading out on to the modern street. It must be nice all the same to face a deserted railway line and have the illusion of residing deep in the country.

The station building at Cults, still with its long platforms and yellow painted woodwork, is in excellent condition and hardly altered, though it is now used by Keiths, the joiners.

Beside the station I spotted my first genuine railway sign *in situ*, a cast-iron notice from the LNER, warning that pedestrians only can use their footpath, and anyone daring to use it with a bicycle, tricycle, hand cart or similar machine would be severely punished. Old railway warnings, with their raised iron letters, always seem so official and frightening. Modern painted signs are so shallow, in every sense. I was surprised no one had pinched it. I looked at it carefully, knowing that they cost £50 at Collector's Corner in London, but I worried that Mr Keith or his joiners might be watching me.

I knocked at the door of the old station. There was no answer, so I went slightly inside a porch way and could hear voices raised. I knocked again and waited but the shouting went on. At last I opened a door at random and went in and there was a little old man, possibly Mr Keith himself, shouting at a man in overalls behind a sort of counter, upbraiding him for some unspecified crime. 'Excuse me, er, I'm walking the railway for a book, could I just, er, look round the station ...?'

'You've come at a verra bad moment,' said the little old man. 'Just wait outside a wee minute.'

He waved imperiously towards a door. I presumed he must be Mr Keith, or someone in charge, so I went through and found myself in some workshops. The old waiting-rooms and even the lavatories had been kept intact, whereas the office part I'd first entered had been part panelled and smartened up. There were carpentry benches and tools all over the place, a strong smell of glue, and pictures of naked ladies with holes in them behind a door, where apparently the apprentices filled in their tea breaks with makeshift games of darts. There were no signs of any workmen, apart from the two arguing in the front office.

I poked around to my satisfaction, admiring the railway remains, then I went back towards the office, but the shouting was still going on. So I left and went back up the line. When I was about a hundred yards away, I happened to look back down the track, which is dead straight, and saw that the little old man had finished shouting and was outside, scratching his head, obviously looking for me. Or had he just imagined that a strange bloke had walked into his office during his argument?

After Cults, the real countryside at last begins and you get a good look at the river Dee which has been flowing quietly to the left of the line, but until now obscured behind roads or houses. The Dee valley has many historic sites and buildings, all worth a detour, if you've got time, several of them connected with the stars of Scottish history, like Mary Queen of Scots, Robert the Bruce, Rob Roy McGregor, but I had too much I wanted to see on the line itself, especially at the Balmoral end.

I did have a quick look at the Shakkin Briggie, an old bridge over the Dee, which can't be missed as it comes in clear view near Cults. It was built in 1837 by a local minister, Dr George Morrison; his church was on the south bank but many of his parishioners lived on the north bank. He feared for their safety when crossing the river by ferry to go to church so he put up the bridge at a cost of £1,450 and left a small sum towards its upkeep. In 1920, however, heavy floods damaged the bridge and the masonry on the south side was swept away. Over the years, the river has altered its course, and what's left of the bridge now leads nowhere. It's a rare example of a nineteenth-century chain suspension bridge and is listed under the Ancient Monuments Act.

Near Peterculter I came across two young workmen, walking home, the first people I'd seen for several miles. One was wearing a blue and white scarf, which made him look like a football supporter, and I remembered the football graffiti on the bridge in Aberdeen. They explained that the three phrases I couldn't understand had not, after all, been football obscenities. SHED was the name of a local teenage gang in Garthdee, the area I'd been passing through at the time, and so was MAS, short for Mastrick, a rival gang from an area some five miles away.

'They're just daft sixteen-year-olds. They beat a few folk up, but that's about all. I thought the gangs had finished, but they must be growing again.' As for Ya Bas, I should have known that. It's general Scottish usage for You Bastards.

I was most impressed by Culter station, or what's left of it. It's been incorporated into a very desirable new estate, with very smart, expensive-looking modern houses, tastefully land-scaped. The station building has gone, but there's the platform and bridge (number 1033) and an old wooden notice board, saying CULTER, in faded blue letters. The name, pronounced Cooter, is short for Peterculter. There are references to the varying forms of Culter in names and legends all over this part of Deeside, dating back to the twelfth century when Knights Templars erected a church on the south side of the river, dedicating it to the Blessed Virgin, hence the name Maryculter. On the north bank, the existing parish church was already dedicated to the Prince of the Apostles – hence Peterculter. Peterculter, which is now a litle town in its own right, and Maryculter, still face each other across the river.

They were still in the process of landscaping the old station site, judging by a workman's hut and a pile of rubble at one side of the line. I spied a little white telegraph pot amongst the rubble. I pulled it out and could make out the initials LNER. My first railway trophy.

Not long after Culter, the Deeside Walk ends and you are on your own for the next thirty miles or so, with as yet no public footpath to follow. I'd done enough walking for one day anyway

Next day, I continued on down the line to Crathes, the site of a famous castle, second only to Balmoral in Deeside popularity, now owned by the National Trust for Scotland. By my counting, there were eighteen stations and halts along the line, used at some time during the history of the railway. Crathes has one of the handful of stations which still stand. I had been told it was now occupied by an engraver from Kent, one of a new influx of craftsmen who have managed to take over two or three of the little stations along the line.

The garden of Crathes station looked at first glance like an industrial tip heap, with spoils everywhere, but on closer inspection I could see they'd all been carefully gathered, grouped in little gatherings, arranged to look 'found'. In the middle of what passed for the lawn was a large mound of bricks, old drain pipes and metal junk which had been arranged in the shape of Crathes Castle.

'An exact replica,' said Malcolm Appleby, coming out to greet me. 'All the towers and turrets are correct to scale. Inside it's my compost heap.' Near his front door was an old green Southern Region signpost, saying *Bromley North*. 'That's to confuse the Germans.'

Mr Appleby is a young man of thirty-four who lives alone in

his railway station, surrounded by hundreds of bits of railway relics and associated industrial remnants, all of them considered valueless, until very recently. He has personally found them all, dug them from fields and sidings, picked them up along the old track. He particularly likes old iron bolts, the kind that held the plates to the sleeper, which he can fashion in his forge to any shape he fancies. 'I make them into lumps of art and sell them at £400 each.' When he does this, he usually adds a few strands of gold to the tops, which explains the price.

He was wearing a long and shapeless multi-coloured jumper which I admired, the sort arty craft stalls in London sell at vast expense, boasting its ethnic origins. 'I've worn it for fifteen years. Whenever I get a hole, I just fill it in with whatever wool comes to hand. There's little of the original left.'

He was sitting one day in 1969 in the Fox public house at Keston, near Bromley in Kent, when someone happened to mention that they knew of a station house in Scotland for rent at £2 a week. He'd recently left the last of the five art colleges which he had attended in turn, most of them for very short stays. He worked out in a flash that £2 a week meant £100 a year, which he could just afford. It would give him space and a base to have his own studio for a year, and so he moved up.

He liked it so much that when he got a chance to buy the empty station itself he managed somehow to get together the sort of money which British Rail required. His sealed bid of £1,607 was accepted; he thought it was a lot, and still does, considering that the station was derelict, but he'd fallen in love with the old railway, and with Deeside, and so he asked his parents for a loan of £1,000. 'They thought I was mad.'

Fifty panes of glass had to be replaced, and the woodwork generally was in a bad state, but the roof was sound. The only real alteration he has made in order to make it habitable (by his own humble and rather unusual standards) was to glaze in the open waiting area, between the two little wings. He needed space and good light for his studio work. He is obviously still in love with his station, and has treated it all with great care, keeping, for example, the little round windows which were a feature of most Deeside stations.

The station, inside and outside, is now his own living railway museum, though he does add other non-railway features, when they come his way. In the garden was a naked lady, wearing only frilly knickers, which turned out to be an old shop window model, once belonging to Watt and Grant, Aberdeen's smart department store, part of the House of Fraser empire.

He has researched the history of his station, and the station-masters and their large families who used to live in the station-master's house, but he has failed to get a contemporary photograph of Crathes in its heyday, though he has come across many of similar Deeside stations, such as Dess and Dinnet, Cults and Culter. (He wrote to me six months later to say he'd got one.)

He was thrilled when he took over Crathes to find the high-topped railway clerk's desk had been left behind and in a dusty drawer he found some old LNER freight tickets marked POTATOES, Shunt With Care labels, and some old ledgers. His prize bit of railway literature, found in the station itself, is a Great North of Scotland poster. LNER relics, of all sorts, are quite easy to acquire these days, though quite expensive, but this was the first GNSR scrap I'd ever seen in the flesh, though I've ogled them in books. The poster announces timetables for a bazaar being held in Aberdeen on 8 December 1892, in aid of the Gordon Highlanders. It was just a torn sheet of paper, but a delight for all railway fans who like to see anything connected with old pre-grouping private lines.

With some difficulty, he cleared a path through his mass of working tools and lifted up the original wooden ticket hatch, to reveal the arch of the old booking office. He has scraped it down carefully and repaired it.

He greatly regrets the recent destruction of Banchory station, the next station down the line, and a much bigger, handsomer one than his. 'Queen Victoria contributed some of her own money towards building it. It was in red granite. A real knockout. A corker of a station, one of the best buildings in Banchory.'

He has his own signal-box, which one day he would like to rebuild, though all that remains is the bottom eight feet or so, which is built of granite blocks, and some metal rods and plates. He found one of his best bits of railway ironwork, part of the original track, in his septic tank. It had been built into the tank at one time to hold it together. He also has a line gauge, a rather rare railway trophy – a four-foot rod of shaped iron, used for checking the distance between the tracks.

His own professional career appears to be thriving, despite his devoting so much time to the old railway. Only one bright flash of modern design caught my eye, amongst all the junk and tat – a Chubb burglar alarm system. I understood the reason for it when he produced a beautifully made necklace, done in delicate gold feathers, which he said was 18 carat gold. He also showed me several sheets of solid silver, which I'd never seen before, raw material for some silver goblets and bowls he was working on. He works in precious metals, as well as iron, and was in the middle of an order to engrave several guns, making intricate shapes with gold inlay.

He expects to live in his remote station for ever. 'I'll not move now. I'm settled in.' He doesn't feel lonely, and says he's never short of visitors or company, but doesn't expect to get married. 'I live a peculiar existence. I don't think anyone else could stand it.'

I then went further down the line to Lumphanan. There's not much there, but it too had its own little railway station and beside its remains stands the Macbeth Arms Inn. Lumphanan's claim to world interest is that it was here that Macbeth was finally defeated and slain, whatever Shakespeare would have us believe.

King Macbeth was in fact a strong and popular Scottish king. He succeeded Duncan after killing him in a fair fight in 1040. He reigned with great success and prosperity for seventeen years, until he was defeated, but not slain, in battle at Dunsinane. He fled north and was finally caught in Lumphanan by Macduff, the Thane of Fife. Macbeth's head was cut off, stuck on a pole and carried to Kincardine O'Neil, beside the Dee. A cairn commemorating Macbeth's death still stands at Lumphanan, quite near the old railway station.

Following the loop of the railway line back to the valley proper, I joined the river and the road again at Aboyne, a very busy little town, well known for its Highland Games held on the green in September.

Aboyne was the terminus of the line from 1859 to 1866 and

they gave it a suitably impressive station. Many local enthusiasts consider the present Aboyne station to have been the handsomest Deeside station. I'd expected to find some run-down, vandalised shell, as I'd heard it had been empty almost fifteen years, since the closure of the line. I was amazed to find it looking so splendid and imposing, more like a Highland castle or hotel than a derelict station. It is built of granite, unlike the little wooden and brick stations I'd seen so far, and has a large round tower at either end with the slates arranged in a fish-scales pattern, like Balmoral itself. When it was opened in 1900 it was considered to be the smartest example of railway station architecture in any country district. For size, it naturally can't compare with the big metropolitan termini, like St Pancras or St Enochs, or with places like York or Carlisle, but shows the same Victorian longing for grandeur, turning even small, countryside railway stations into things of classical beauty and stature.

On close inspection, it was obviously well and truly empty, though well and truly boarded up to keep out even the stoutest vandals. I walked down the empty platforms, noticing that the clockface was still intact, showing the maker's name, Alexander Hill, Aberdeen. The John Menzies newspaper stall was also boarded up, but looked as if it could still be used. The pillars supporting the platform roof were in excellent condition, the flower decorations at the top still bright green, as if they'd been newly painted.

There's a row of affluent-looking shops, all very clean and county, opposite the station, and I went across to find someone who might know what was happening to the station. Outside George Strachan's very smart grocery store (By Appointment to Her Majesty the Queen) I talked to an elderly man who was pulling out the shop blinds to preserve the Fortnum and Mason-style delicacies from the hot Highland sun.

'Dr Beeching made a terrible mistake. Look at the price of petrol today. It's a blooming shame. The trains from Aboyne to Ballater used to be crowded every Sunday. It was so handy for a day out. We used to use it for the shop. As a nipper one of my earliest jobs was putting parcels of food on the train to be sent to Ballater.

'The porters at the station took great pride in its appearance.

[65]

They had baskets of flowers all over the place. I don't know what they're going to do with it now. Those old people's homes over there have been put up by the council on the site of old station buildings, but the station itself has just been left.

'In the last few years of the line they introduced battery trains, the first in Britain. We called them the sputnik trains. Because they made a spluttery sort of noise, I suppose.

'As a boy I always used to come to the station to watch the royal family going through. Everyone did. It didn't stop of course – it was non-stop from Aberdeen to Ballater. All the level crossings were manned right along the line and no other trains were allowed. I remember them inspecting the tunnel outside Aboyne before it arrived. It was a great sight, the royal coaches all shining, with big double doors. There was always a coat of arms at the front, in blue. Aye, they were grand days.'

After Aboyne, the line goes past an old airfield, now used by a gliding club, then at last it enters real Highland country. There's a sign on the road nearby to tell you that the Highlands Begin Here. Every tourist can then get his camera out. You are suddenly in wild moorland, surrounded by a sea of wild heather, in an area called the old Muir (meaning moor) of Dinnet. I could see snow-capped mountains ahead and tall pine forests across the river banks.

The last few miles to Ballater, from about Cambus O'May old station, was easy walking as this final stretch is council property. On the way, just beside the road, is a little cottage with its sign outside, Cutaway Cottage. It is pretty obvious how it got its name as you can see where a corner of the cottage was knocked off to make way for the railway. When this part of the line was being built, in the 1860s, they didn't want to destroy the cottage. Having sliced a bit off, it then became a home for the lengthsman working on the line. It must have been a pretty noisy cottage to live in, with trains slipping past, only a foot away from your outside wall.

The zenith of the railway, judging by old timetables, was from about the 1890s to 1914 when six passenger trains a day, plus one express and two goods, steamed the whole length of the line, from Aberdeen to Ballater, with extra trains on

Wednesdays and Saturdays. In addition, there was a more frequent service serving just the eastern end, taking commuters from Culter into Aberdeen. On summer Saturdays, Culter station, which is now that bit of landscaped suburbia, with only the station name surviving, had thirty-five up trains and thirty-five down trains.

Cutaway Cottage, before the railway took it over, was formerly the old ferry inn, a refreshment place for people crossing the river and making for the old Deeside turnpike road. The river Dee, which is still liable to flood after heavy winter snows, is said to have risen so high in 1829 that a full-grown trout was found in the plate rack of the inn.

The last stretch of the walk isn't very exciting, as the track itself is flat and rather dusty, though this is in comparison with the incredible scenery all around. You want to be up on the hillsides, or even higher and skiing on the mountain tops, not stuck down in the plain on a little man-made path, especially when as you near Ballater the line runs into a new estate of bungalows. But then comes the big treat – Ballater station, still there in all its regal glory.

Architecturally, it is related to the little stations I'd seen, such as Crathes, rather than the granite castle style of Aboyne, but of course it is much bigger. It had to be. It was the grand ceremonial station for all the famous arrivals and departures, with its own special and very private royal waiting-room.

The Czar of Russia, Nicholas ii, and the Czarina (who was Queen Victoria's granddaughter) arrived here on 22 September 1896 for a holiday at Balmoral with the royal family. And what an occasion that was. There are contemporary prints which show the massed detachment of the Black Watch, one hundred strong, all in kilts, who welcomed the Russian guests at the station and marched beside their coaches all the way to Balmoral in a torchlight procession.

Such a heavy display of uniformed troops was not simply out of courtesy to the distinguished visitors but because of fears that the whole visit would turn into a diplomatic incident. The Czarina herself was popular enough, but important sections of the British press, local and national, were attacking the Czar for being a tyrant in his own country, someone we shouldn't give hospitality to. It sounds a very modern political incident. Such things never seem to change.

The local council in Aberdeen walked right into the row by agreeing to lend the Great North of Scotland Railway an engine and a dynamo (£5 hire for the day) so that they could light Ballater station by electricity, especially for the great arrival.

'When Aberdeen comes to its senses we hope it will be ashamed of the ridiculous part it has played over this Czar business,' stormed a local paper, the *Bon Accord*. 'When the Czar is at home we do not hesitate to call him a tyrant ... then in heaven's name why, when a man with whom we have no sympathy, touches our city on the way to see his grand mother in law, why do the town council play the hypocrite and fête he whom they at other times curse?'

In the event, the Russian visit passed off without incident. Nobody threw anything nasty, marched with placards, chained themselves to any railings, or whatever the 1890s version of a demo might have been, and the party returned to the railway station without any fuss on 3 October. As they left Ballater station, the band of the Black Watch bade them farewell by playing the Russian national hymn. Ah, stirring times.

Today, the station still stands, but only just, having recently been saved from destruction. It has lain empty, and been vandalised, for many years, but now the local council (Kincardine and Deeside District) have at last found new uses for it, so their director of planning informed me when I wrote to him. They are already using part of it themselves, as a district office where people can pay their rates; part is being used as a restaurant; the eastmost portion is soon to be demolished to make way for a 'small advance factory unit', whatever that may be. The goods yard and track, which is now full of debris, is going to be laid out as a parking and picnic area.

From the front, the station still looks terrific, with the cream woodwork in good condition. Most of the fancy wooden eaves are still intact. Most surprising of all, many of the stained-glass windows are still intact. The part now a restaurant – which had absolutely no customers when I walked in, despite it being Easter holidays – has letters in its stained-glass windows, saying Luncheons, Dining Room, Teas.

I went into the part used by the council, and queued up
behind an old woman who was paying her rates of £42, and
asked the lady behind the counter if I could look around. She
was a bit dubious, with council money to protect, but she let
me in. At last, I was stepping in genuine royal footsteps. This
was Queen Victoria's own private royal waiting-room. By some
miracle, very little had been changed.

I examined the internal glass doors and windows which were
dripping with elaborate royal symbols. The lady helped me
pick out shamrocks, thistles and roses, but we couldn't quite
make out some very ornate lettering. It seemed to read GIR,
which didn't make sense. I would have expected it to be GNSR,
for the original railway company. It most probably was
GVR for George v. (It couldn't have been George i as he was
a hundred years too early for the railway.)

The walls and ceiling were equally ornate, with gold inlay
and lots of carving. I don't suppose there's a more luxurious
local council office in the country. But where was Queen Victoria's own private lavatory? This was her waiting-room. Even
a queen, when waiting around, has to be provided for.

It's just been sold, so the council lady told me, to a Ballater
hotel, the Loriston, just around the corner, across the green. I
said I'd make it my next stop. I couldn't miss that.

Outside the station, I admired the front once again and then
noticed, high up, on the building opposite, a sign saying 'Albert
Memorial Hall'. On the corner of the building, carved in stone,
were lots of fancy-looking letters, coats of arms and other in-
scriptions, some beginning to fade, but some I could read very
clearly, even with my tired eyes.

'A PRINCE INDEED. Above all the titles, a Household
word, hereafter through all time. ALBERT THE GOOD.'

It must have been a bit of a mouthful for the stonemason. I
hope he got the punctuation right. It reads more like a transla-
tion from the Latin than a piece of household English, but I
take it to mean they were praising Albert for being one of
nature's princes, a frequent observation made by loyal subjects
in Victorian days. We do owe Prince Albert a lot, for his creation
of Balmoral and his lovely royal railway line.

I stood in the main square of Ballater for some time,

looking up high to the surrounding snow-capped peaks, thinking I was in an Alpine village. Ballater is in a little alluvial plain, very flat and neat and ordered. They'd had the first tourist rush of the year over the Easter weekend as the weather had been unbelievably sunny. Every shop was sold out and every shopkeeper exhausted. I failed to buy any local maps as they'd all gone, or any books on Deeside.

Like all little towns near a royal palace, such as Windsor or Sandringham, there was a generous sprinkling of little shops boasting royal coats of arms. By Appointment to the Queen for Fishing Tackle, Cakes and Bread, Outfitters.

I went to find the Loriston Hotel, which was just beside the green. It hadn't got a royal appointment, at least not so far. Perhaps they never will, depending on what they do with the royal loo.

I asked for the manager, but he wasn't in. The hotel hadn't properly opened for the season. (The Scottish tourist season opens in May full time, not from Easter as in England.) The girl on the reception desk had started only that day and she looked amazed, and then giggled, when I said I wanted to see Queen Victoria's lavatory. She'd never heard of it. She called for another receptionist who said yes, the hotel had bought it, but I couldn't see it just now. It was locked up in a store room and she hadn't got a key. 'I have seen it, though. It's very posh. There's a big old wooden seat with it, and cushions. It's sort of white and blue porcelain. I don't know what the manager's going to do with it. Perhaps set it up in the bar as a show piece.'

After wallowing in so many royal connections, however remote, since leaving Aberdeen, I decided to finish off Royal Deeside by going to Balmoral itself, about seven more miles up the Dee. At one time in the 1860s there was a plan to continue the railway from Ballater up to Braemar, building a little station at Crathie, beside the church the royal family still attend. There were lengthy hearings in the House of Commons and much public and private discussion, but the plans for extension were finally killed. Queen Victoria was not amused by the thought of having the hordes right on her doorstep, even if they would be on the other side of the river.

Balmoral Castle is a completely Victorian creation. There

was an old building on the estate when Albert bought it in 1851, but he and Queen Victoria built a brand-new castle which was completed in 1857. It is probably one of the best-known buildings in Britain, even by millions who've never been there, as it appears in all those luridly coloured picture books of the royal family. Every local shop sells Balmoral Castle picture postcards, with or without the royals posing in front, with or without their kilts and sporrans.

Balmoral is the ultimate in Scottish baronial style and is indeed a splendid sight. Glamis Castle, near Forfar, the Queen Mother's ancestral home, is perhaps a more attractive *building*, because of its warmer coloured sandstone, but the total effect of Balmoral is magnificent. Its setting, from the immediate and marvellously cared for gardens and estate, to the beautiful banks of the nearby river, and then in the background the towering mountains, is utterly Hollywood. You couldn't create a more wonderful position, if you were starting from scratch with unlimited money. The fact that there's a main road, just a mile away across the river, is easily forgotten as it's screened by fir trees.

The grounds are open in the summer, when the royal family are not in residence, and the gardeners work towards an autumn show, when the family arrive. Deeside is extremely dry, with gardeners often praying for rain rather than shine. The royal family are always out of doors when they stay at Balmoral, whatever the weather. They can manage a twenty-mile walk, round the 42,000 acre estate, without ever once being spied on by the public. What a relief that must be.

I went through the gardens and down to the river and found some little iron plates in the ground, marking where high tides over the centuries have tried to creep up the two hundred yards or so and catch the castle unawares, perhaps with trout to drop on the royal plate rack. The highest mark appeared to be 24 January 1939, when the river got about a third of the way to the castle.

I got back to my hotel that night, the Tulloch Lodge, near Ballater, by walking back along the railway line. As I was putting on a collar and tie for dinner, as it's a terribly respectable hotel, shaking off my dusty railway clothes, I noticed that inside the wardrobe was fixed a discreet little notice. 'James Allan and Sons, Aberdeen, Cabinet Makers and Upholsterers to the Queen.' I suppose when you walk a royal railway you have to expect to meet royal connections in almost every little corner.

5 🚂 The Cockermouth, Keswick and Penrith Railway

A WALK THROUGH THE LAKE DISTRICT

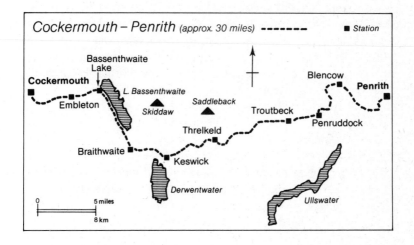

THE COCKERMOUTH, Keswick and Penrith Railway Company had the distinction of being the only railway company to get its line right *through* the Lake District. The Maryport and Carlisle was bigger and more powerful, but it went round the west coast. The Furness line, which started round Barrow in 1846, and had a very long and distinguished history, dominated the south of Lakeland, but it never got past Coniston or reached the heart of Lakeland. The Lancaster and Carlisle, also begun in 1846, did sterling work in forging a route over Shap, but that was well to the east of the Lakes proper, as was the Midland Railway's remarkable route from Settle to Carlisle.

It was the mountain mass of central Lakeland which kept the railways at bay, but so did the hand of man. William Wordsworth, Lakeland's greatest son, raised an enormous outcry when the first railway to penetrate anywhere near the Lake District, the Kendal and Windermere, which opened in 1847, had the audacity to contemplate pushing its line right into the Lakes, reaching Wordsworth's own doorstep at Rydal. There were even thoughts of going right on, up and over Dunmail Raise and reaching Keswick, following the old pack-horse road which Coleridge used when he walked over to see the Wordsworths at Grasmere.

Wordsworth soon put a stop to that, writing letters to the papers and producing a poem which has been used by preservationists everywhere, when they see modern man about to spoil something. 'Is then no nook of English ground secure from rash assault?'

Wordsworth wasn't against railways, as such. He travelled on them frequently, all round the country, across to Newcastle from Carlisle, down to Birmingham and London, and wrote about them in other poems in admiring terms. It was the thought of one disturbing his own peace and quiet that really alarmed him, though of course he didn't admit to that reason. He maintained it was because he didn't want the Lakes overwhelmed and ruined by hordes of people from Lancashire on day trips. The working classes anyway, so he thought, or even the shopkeepers, would not appreciate the Lakes. They were for gentle folk of taste and should be kept unsullied.

In the event, the railway stopped at Lake Windermere, but what Wordsworth feared came to pass. Almost overnight the tiny lakeside hamlet of Birthwaite, where the railway ended, was turned into a roaring tourist resort, with hotels springing up everywhere – and so was born a brand-new town called Windermere, still the biggest town in the Lakes. (Its permanent population, including Bowness, is 8,500 – Keswick's is 5,000.) Throughout every summer season since then, the Kendal and Windermere line, which was later absorbed by the London and North Western, has disgorged hundreds of thousands of visitors. It is still going strong and provides a perfect entrance to the Lake District.

The Cockermouth, Keswick and Penrith line, however, which was started much later, opening in 1865, managed to bisect the Lakes, travelling from east to west. (The Windermere line would have continued south to north.) Admittedly, it took the fairly easy northern way, going from Cockermouth round the shores of Bassenthwaite to Keswick, then through the Threlkeld valley to Penrith.

The primary reason for its construction was to provide a more direct route from the South Durham coalfields to the newly emerging iron industry of West Cumberland. One difficulty which had hindered the local iron works was that at the time West Cumbrian coal was not suitable for iron smelting.

There was some fierce opposition from many vested interests, notably the Maryport and Carlisle Railway who had been taking most of the iron and coke traffic on their line, round the coast, but the new company got its Act of Parliament in 1861. The contractor was Boulton and Son of Newcastle who tendered to do the job for £267,000. The engineer was Thomas Bouch, a native Cumbrian who came from the village of Thursby and had gone to school in Carlisle. He started as an apprentice on the Lancaster and Carlisle Railway and went on to make a name for himself by specialising in low-cost light railways.

The Cockermouth, Keswick and Penrith line was finished on time but there were delays due to the final costs which had risen by £10,000 and there was a long-drawn-out dispute with the contractor. When the line eventually opened to passengers on 2 January 1865, it was decided by the company that to save money the opening would not be accompanied by 'any great public demonstration'. In those days, most railway openings were an excuse for local celebrations.

Thomas Bouch is best remembered today for one of his later engineering works, the Tay Bridge. This collapsed during a gale in December 1879 killing seventy-five passengers and the crew of a train. It was a national disaster and the blame was laid on many heads, but alas for Bouch, he was singled out as the main villain. He retired soon afterwards to Moffat, heartbroken by the disaster, and died a year later in 1880.

His Cockermouth line was a great success. In all, there were ten stations along the route – Cockermouth, Embleton, Bass Lake, Braithwaite, Keswick, Threlkeld, Troutbeck, Penruddock, Blencow, Penrith.

Like the Windermere line, it enjoyed tremendous popularity with tourists. In these mid-Victorian boom years, the Lake District became a popular holiday area for millions of people, partly as a result of the lives and writings of the Lake Poets.

In its first year, 1865, the Keswick line (I'll call it that as C.K. and P. looks so impersonal) carried 75,000 passengers. By 1882 this had shot up to 225,000. At the same time as the opening of the line, they built the impressive-looking Keswick Hotel, right beside the station buildings which also contained the headquarters of the railway company.

By the 1920s and 30s, road transport was beginning to take away most of its passengers. There were drastic staff cuts, stations closed or became unmanned, and the end finally came in 1972. The line became a scene of further bitter arguments when it was proposed to build the A66 trunk road, from Penrith to Keswick, running parallel to, and even using the old railway route for many miles. It was considered sacrilegious to have a veritable motorway polluting the heart of Lakeland, with cars and lorries hurtling through the Lakes at up to 70 mph non-stop. But, it all came to pass. Those who thought the little single-track steam train was noisy should listen to the juggernauts on the A66 today.

I went first to Cockermouth, not knowing whether there would be any railway relics left to see. Welcome to the Birthplace of William Wordsworth, so the signs say, but there's nothing to direct you to the old railway. As he fought Lake District railways for so long, Wordsworth would probably be quite pleased to be told that the Cockermouth, Keswick and Penrith finally collapsed.

Cockermouth itself is far from run down and is a thriving little market town. It's just outside the Lake District National Park boundary, which makes a spiteful loop as if to deliberately avoid it, and the Cumbria Tourist Board people are always trying to draw attention to its attractions, hoping to shift a few thousand of the trippers from the usual spots, like Grasmere and Keswick, to Cockermouth and the West Cumbrian coast, but with little luck. Cockermouth has a few caffs and tourist shops, but nothing compared with Keswick and Windermere. It is very much a real town, with real industries, particularly agricultural.

The station had gone completely with not a brick in sight. It's now a flattened wasteland, most of it being used as a car park, though there weren't many cars in sight, just a few tired buses and some sort of works used by an agricultural machinery firm, Oliver and Snowdon. At the entrance to the car park is a triumphal war memorial which must have looked rather fitting when the station was here, standing guard over the railway buildings, but now it stands alone in dusty isolation. On top it has a winged lady figure, holding a laurel wreath. I ran my eye down the names of the sons of Cockermouth killed in the Second World War, noting the preponderance of local names, like four Hetheringtons and three Irvings but only one Wordsworth.

The old track leads from the car park straight on to a concrete railway bridge where I stopped, as usual, to study the graffiti, wondering how they came to put up such a horrible bridge in such a pretty place, and so recently as well, judging by its condition. The concrete provides a good surface for the aerosol brigade and I could easily make out 'Sex Pistols' and 'Stiff Little Fingers'. They don't have a League football team in

Cockermouth, nor in Workington any more, so the lads apparently have to make do with pop groups, however dated.

I nearly didn't look over the bridge, as the high concrete sides were so ugly, but I climbed up for a quick glimpse and there below was the river Cocker looking exceedingly sylvan and Wordsworthian. This is the stream where he used to swim as a little boy, going naked like a savage, so he said in *The Prelude*.

I clambered down the bank to the Cocker itself where a couple of boys were fishing with little toy nets. The bridge is supported by three large stone pillars, no doubt the original parts of the bridge, whereas the concrete slabs on top look very twentieth-century. Under the bridge I met a lady with a dog.

'The railway station was lovely,' she said. 'It's stupid what they did to it. And the money they spent on this bridge! They rebuilt it just after the war – not long before they closed it for ever.'

As a young girl in the 1930s she used to travel on the railway every morning from Cockermouth to Keswick, catching the 6.45 there and the 5.45 back. 'You were lucky to get any work in them days. There was nothing in Cockermouth. I worked at the Pencil works in Keswick, varnishing pencils. The trains were always so crowded in those days.'

As an even younger girl, she was taken as a treat for the day into Keswick on the railway. 'I used to love playing on Keswick station. Oh, it was a lovely station, even nicer than Cockermouth's. The Keswick Hotel was right beside it, with its own entrance, and they used to have this conservatory. I don't know if it's still there. When no one was looking, I used to sneak into the hotel, have a look round, then sneak out again. It was marvellous. I loved to see the fine ladies in fancy hats and men smoking big cigars. It was the smell of those cigars that used to appeal to me. I thought it was all wonderful.

'I don't know what's happened to Keswick station either. All they seem to do these days is pull places down. Idiots, all of them.'

I promised I would investigate when I got to Keswick, but by the look of the Cockermouth devastations, I held out little hope.

The first station on the line after Cockermouth was at Embleton but this is now on the main A66 trunk road which has eaten up all traces of the old station. There's not much pleasure in trying to walk the route from Embleton to Keswick, though it can be clearly seen, unless you want to run the risk of being run over, or deafened. I noticed a house at Embleton called Station House, right beside the main road, which had railway-ish green-painted eaves, presumably the old station-master's house.

I really must find an adjective to describe railway things. If it's to do with the army you can say military, naval for the navy, or clerical for the church, but how do you describe something pertaining to railways? Railwayanic, railwayesque, railic? British Rail must have been faced with a similar problem when they set up their wonderful shop which sells second-hand railway goods at Euston. They avoided the problem by naming it Collector's Corner, which tells you absolutely nothing. No wonder people can never find it.

Bass Lake station, where the railway turned sharp right to follow the shore of Bassenthwaite Lake, is still there. It's a wonder the new road didn't destroy it. In fact there are several buildings – the station itself, empty but in excellent condition, along with the station-master's house and another railway house, both of which appeared to be occupied.

I walked along the old platform beside the empty station and poked around, looking through the boarded-up windows, admiring the cream and maroon paintwork. I could see some railway platform seats inside, a notice saying 'Ladies' and the booking hall which looked untouched since the last railway clerk moved out. A handwritten notice in one window said 'Premises Sold', so perhaps it is going to be saved after all.

It must have been a beautiful train ride, steaming right along the edge of Bass Lake, looking across to the towering mass of the Skiddaw range. If you hop over the wall from the main road and drop down on to the old track, choosing a suitable lull in the traffic, it can seem a magical spot, with only the gentle lapping of the lake a few feet away. Tennyson had his honeymoon on Bassenthwaite, on the other side, and he had the lake in mind when he was writing *Morte d'Arthur*, thinking of its misty edges when he had Excalibur being thrown into the depths. All I could see were some bright yachts, sailing on the northern shores. Bassenthwaite is today one of the most popular sailing lakes in Cumbria.

I eventually worked my way into Keswick, losing the old track which bends slightly north as it enters the town, under the slopes of Skiddaw, going through what is now a school and then a junk yard for old cars.

I had lunch in Keswick in a cheerful and very reasonable restaurant called the Yan Tan Tether. This is how the old shepherds used to count their sheep, in a sort of Cumbrian Norse for One Two Three. So many of the eating places in Keswick are pretty awful, turning out the usual tourist fry-ups, so it's a pleasure to find a place doing proper food and good salads.

I went into several book shops but was unable to find anything about Keswick station or the old railway. For such an interesting little railway, not much seems to have been written about it. I failed to track down any old published memories, even when later I wrote a letter to the letters page of the *Cumberland Evening News*. Most old railways, if you look around long enough, have had several specialist books written about them, if only private publications, published locally.

I then went up the hill, past Fitz Park, towards the old station. I wasn't even sure if it would still be there, but it was, though boarded at the front with a notice saying Keswick Model Railway. I couldn't see a way of getting in so I went to the Keswick Hotel which is just beside it.

The station and the hotel dominate the little hill, looking down and over Keswick, sitting proudly over everyone and everything, though in the case of the station, it hasn't much to be proud of any more. But Keswick Hotel looks suitably exclusive and affluent, in a quiet, comfortable sort of way. Posh London hotels are somehow a bit menacing, as if there are unseen eyes watching you, waiting to catch you out, and then chuck you out. Posh provincial hotels are usually as dozy inside as outside, with no one to accost you and make you feel you don't belong.

Keswick Hotel was built by the railway, next door to the railway station which contained the headquarters of the railway company. Today it is owned by Trust House Forte. I went to reception and asked if there was a hotel brochure, but all they could give me was their 1980 tariff – double room with bathroom £29, suite £60.

The girl had no idea that this had once been a railway hotel, and had never heard of the Cockermouth, Keswick and Penrith Railway, and why should she? She looked about eighteen. There were no railway relics in the hotel, as far as she knew.

Railway hotels are worth a book in themselves, though no one seems to have done a full study of them. They were often integral parts of the station, or built soon afterwards, with the same longings for grandeur, ranging from the architecturally magnificent, as at St Pancras or York (Queen Victoria stayed with several of her children at York's railway hotel in 1854 and allowed it from then on to become the Royal Railway Hotel), to the architecturally rather mad. Any visitors to Carlisle, perhaps before plunging south to explore the Keswick line, should have a look at its railway station. It was built in 1847 and for some reason, best known to its architect, Sir William Tite, has a mock-Tudor front. Next door, the hotel (now called the County Hotel), built in 1856, is trying to pretend it's really a French chateau.

I had a look around the public rooms of the Keswick Hotel, showing the sort of cheek I wouldn't have attempted at the Connaught, poking my head into the bar and the lounge. On a wall near the main hall I found a relief map of the Lakes which once belonged to the London Midland and Scottish Railway and showed all their routes, a memento of the company which took over the Keswick line, before British Rail.

I wandered into a very attractive sun lounge, a sort of conservatory with glass roof and walls, and I realised this must lead directly on to the old station as the lady at Cockermouth had told me. It enabled the cigar-smoking guests at Keswick Hotel to have their own private access to Keswick station. I tried the door connected to the station, but it was locked.

On the glass doors and windows of the conservatory were some very handsome stained-glass portraits of famous artists, Jan Van Eyck, Van Dyck, Rubens, Velasquez, Veronese, Peter Lely, Godfrey Kneller. I couldn't work out why the railway had decided to celebrate so many artists, most of them seventeenth century. If they had portrayed Stephenson or Brunel, I could have understood it. Perhaps when they built the Keswick Hotel they were trying to culturally outdo their rival the Royal Oak, for many years Keswick's smartest place. It has the Lake Poets portrayed on the stained-glass windows of the dining room.

I'd seen bits of the old station platform through the conservatory door, so when I left the hotel, I went back to the station and managed to get through a coal merchant's yard to the left of it. A coalman came out of a little hut, looking defiantly sooty, and asked what I wanted. I said I was trying to get on to the old railway line and he said 'That's fine'. Would that all new residents of railway property were so easy-going.

Keswick station was a terrific surprise, and a great delight. I hadn't expected it to be quite so grand, for such a little town. It has an enormous glass and wrought-iron canopy over the entire length of the main platform – over eighty paces long, as I found when I stepped it out. It looked like some giant aristocratic greenhouse built by Paxton for the Duke of Devonshire. Naturally, almost all the glass was broken, the platform dangerously littered, and all the station windows vandalised.

I came to one door into the old booking office which was open so I explored inside, pulling open old drawers, looking under counters, searching in fireplaces for any treasures, but I didn't discover anything. All I found on the site was an LMS pot insulator from the top of a railway telegraph pole. This was outside the station building, in a pile of old motor car remains. My second trophy.

At the end of the platform I came to Keswick Hotel's own private entrance, which looked in good condition, even though some of the stained-glass windows are well within vandalising distance. I thought again of that lady in Cockermouth as a little girl, sneaking in to the hotel, just to get a whiff of top-drawer life.

I carried on walking along the platform, which continues for another hundred yards, well after the covered part, being raised in some parts as if on stilts, past some gas lamp-posts in good condition.

Keswick station and a few miles of the old line have recently been bought by the National Park Planning Board. I contacted their chief officer later, Michael Taylor, and he confirmed that there are plans to turn the station into a theatre (as a home for Keswick's Century Theatre). It has also been suggested that there might be room for swimming baths, and a conference centre. It all sounds very commendable and I hope one day it happens. It is a magnificent building and well deserves some imaginative redevelopment.

Leaving the station, heading for Troutbeck, I came to a rather rickety wooden bridge over the river Greta, a long, swaying bridge which they'll have to spend some money on, if they're going to encourage the public to walk it. It is obviously frequently used, despite the gaping holes in the slats and the lack of iron railings in many places. There were pretty views to the left, along the Greta, but in the middle of the river I could see a large metal farm gate, rather new-looking. They must have some very strong vandals in the Keswick area.

After the river bridge, I came to a white post marked '$\frac{1}{4}$' which I thought at first was a gradient post, but realised the line was flat. I then decided it must have meant a quarter of a mile to Keswick station, or perhaps twelve and a quarter from Penrith.

On a little bridge over a public footpath, there were some boys lying in wait, a pile of stones beside them, watching the path below. I could see a group of kids coming towards them, winding their way down towards the bridge from a council estate. Should I say, 'Now now, boys, don't be horrid'? I might get a mouthful, or the stones thrown at me instead. So I averted my gaze to the left and admired the slopes of Latrigg, the steep first rung up Skiddaw. On the map, Latrigg is very small, nothing compared with its big brother, but when I once climbed it, going straight up it from the road, I found it more tiring than Skiddaw.

I could hear further shouts of children ahead, but this time joyous ones, singing and dancing and laughing. I followed the cries and looked down into a back garden where eight little girls of about seven were playing pass the parcel, all in their best party clothes. The mother was standing at a window, leaning through into the house and turning off a record player for the parcel to stop. I could hear the laughter of the little girls, long after they had gone from sight.

'Excuse me, have you seen Burnswood Farm?' A youth with a strong Geordie accent was standing in front of me, along with another tough-looking youth, both carrying rucksacks. I hadn't noticed them on the overgrown line ahead of me. I studied my map, but could find no farm with that sort of name. They'd been told, so they said, that it had a camp site. They'd arrived by bus from Newcastle that morning and since then had spent four hours wandering round Keswick. All the camp sites were full and wouldn't take them. I suggested they should walk up Latrigg. They could find a sheltered spot there, well away from everyone.

'We want to stay in Keswick. For the drinking, you see. We want to pitch war tent near a pub. We're just here for the weekend. Me Mother thinks I've come for the fresh air but we hope to get alcoholic poisoning. All we've got so far is sore legs.'

They went off in the direction of Keswick, laughing at their own wit.

Keswick these days is a nightmare for road users. It can take hours to get into the town in the height of the summer, and when you've managed that, the car parks are usually full. Even on the outskirts, trying to by-pass the town, it can be even more annoying. The dreaded A66 trunk road, deserting the simple railway route, carves up the fringes of Keswick with strange roundabouts and flyovers which seem to take you at great speed in the opposite direction from the one you want. Many Lake District maps don't show the new road, or the roundabouts, so the confusion for motorists can be endless.

I was thinking what a pleasure it was to be walking out of Keswick, in peace and rural seclusion, when I came face to face with a brand-new concrete flyover. As flyovers go, it was quite spectacular, soaring in one leap over the old railway, a road and the river Greta, but it was the last thing I wanted to stop and admire. I couldn't get over the screaming trunk road as the fences were too high. I'd lost the railway line.

It took some time, and a lot of messing around, trying to avoid some new houses which now sit on part of the line, trying to avoid walking on the trunk road, trying to work out where the old railway had gone. From an old map I could see that the railway had stuck religiously to the Greta Gorge for several

In 1963 Dr Beeching put his foot down firmly – and that was the beginning of the end of the branch lines. In 1955, we had 19,000 miles of railway lines. Today, mainly as a result of the Beeching Report, we have only 11,000 miles. The closures were mourned by many, but it does mean that we now have 8,000 miles of empty railway lines, perfect for exploration.

Dr Beeching in 1962, visiting the Bluebell Railway, Sussex.

Workmen on an iron girder bridge south of Leicester, on the Great Central, taken around 1897 shortly before completion of the line.

One problem with old railway buildings is what to do with them. Pocklington School, York, found a magnificent solution – they turned the disused Pocklington Railway Station into their sports hall.

A Pride of Locomotive Heroes, lined up at the National Railway Museum
in York.

Queen Victoria's saloon, used by the LNWR, 1869, on show at York.

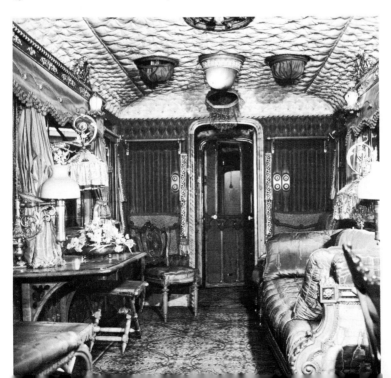

Above: Royal Deeside.
Edward VIII (just prior to his
abdication) and the Duke of
York, at Ballater Station,
1936.

Below: Part of the disused
Deeside Railway which has
been converted into a public
walkway, and the old
Pitfodels Station - now a
private house.

Keswick Railway Station, 1966, now disused, on the old Cockermouth, Keswick and Penrith Railway.

Hadlow Road Station on the Wirral Way, Merseyside, the best-preserved old railway station in the country.

Wye Valley Railway, Wales: Four smart railway men, St Briavels Station, 1923. Charles Fox, signal porter, is on the right.

Mr Fox today.

Below left: Tintern Station, preserved, for walkers and picnics.

Below right: Monmouth Troy Station, disused, left for the lorries.

Christopher Somerville outside Hook Norton Brewery on the old Banbury–Cheltenham line.

The old viaduct at Shepton Mallet, on the Somerset–Dorset line, landscaped by Showerings, the makers of Babycham.

Intrepid railway walker, H. Davies,
at Highgate Tunnel on the old Ally
Pally line.

Alexandra Palace Station, 1932, with the Palace looming behind.

miles after leaving Keswick, now and again criss-crossing it. They must have spent a fortune landscaping the river area when they put up the flyover, altering all the contours. Eventually I got rid of the new road and hit the tranquillity of the old railway line once again.

The final section of the line, from Keswick to Penrith, is by far the best for railway walks. The Cockermouth end was closed as early as April 1966 but the Keswick–Penrith section was used till 1972. There are many more railway relics to be seen and the walking is easier and prettier.

There's still a good chance that a lot of it will one day become a public pathway, at least the bit from Keswick to Threlkeld. The National Park people are still in negotiation, despite some opposition from local landowners. One of the big problems is the cost of maintenance. There are nine metal bridges over the Greta, all very costly to care for, or even to destroy.

Perhaps the best bit of railway engineering in the final stretch is the Mosedale Viaduct which for years I have viewed from afar when climbing the nearby fells. It can be seen so clearly from the slopes and even the top of Saddleback. I'd never known quite where it was, or its name.

We approached it along the track from Birkett Field and it proved to be an enormous viaduct, twelve arches long, and about a hundred feet high, yet it goes over a rather puny little stream, the Mosedale Beck. (Which is why I've called it the Mosedale Viaduct, though it might have another name.)

There were no notices saying 'Keep off', no fences, no hint that it was private, no evidence that it was dangerous or disintegrating, so we walked boldly across. At the far end, I found a few bricks marked Clifton, perhaps from a brickworks near Clifton, Workington, which had fallen off. As you walk over the viaduct, the left-hand side has a brick wall to stop you falling off while the other side has a simple open-work iron railing. Why did they do them differently? Did they want to hide the trains from the sight of people in the valley? Were they saving money? The line was originally built as a single track, so perhaps when they doubled it, they changed the construction of the bridge.

My fourteen-year-old son, Jake, who had joined me for this

section, decided to jump down and explore the steep sides of the beck, determined to cross it. He gave a great shout and I saw him, a tiny figure, far below, struggling to drag something from the beck. I went down and he'd found a heavy chunk of iron. We washed it and it turned out to be an old iron chair which held the rails in place. On it was marked LMS 1935. What a discovery! As we dragged it back, we found another one, embedded in mud under the arches, and then another. Presumably some workmen, who'd been given the job of lifting the rails in 1972, had dropped them over the viaduct into the stream, by mistake or by fooling around. We counted nine in the end, buried in the mud. We were content to struggle home with one, so the rest are still there. Don't all rush.

All along the final section we kept coming across large and very ornate iron posts at the sides of the railway line. They appeared to be some sort of patent device for holding the railway fence straight and taut, each a mass of cogs and levers for tightening. I could make out the name Francis Mason of Liverpool, but there was no clue to their age. The ground underfoot was basically the original ballast, showing how recently this end of the line had become disused, though in patches grass had been growing.

We came to a railwayman's hut, with its walls and roof intact. There were lots of iron rods and wires thrown around outside, including several telegraph insulators still screwed to the wooden batons, stamped LMS 1924 and 1925, one of which I unscrewed as another souvenir. We even found a short length of the original rail, rather rusty, but too heavy to carry.

Jake, being terribly brave, went into the hut, which wasn't difficult as the door was broken down, and poked around inside. He gave a loud yell when he touched an old tin and some dangerous-looking brown liquid poured out, splashing his hands. It could be rat poison, Dad. Will I have to go to hospital, Dad? I turned over the tin with a stick and it said Beans and Sausages.

We passed several bridges, all in good condition, with the main steel girder telling the world, or that part of it which still walks the line, that the bridges were made by Pratchitt Brothers, Carlisle, 1892. My father-in-law once worked with that firm as a fitter. He would have liked to have seen the bridges, but they were just a bit big to take home as souvenirs.

The track was now straight for a while, across the broad valley towards Penrith, with clear views either side, little sign of embankments, and terrific scenery all around, with Clough Head to the right and Saddleback and Souther Fell to the left.

My wife had refused to walk the line with us, saying she preferred to walk the fells any time. She finds old railways boring. I've tried to tell her that it's industrial history, not just a nice walk. Then there's all the flora and fauna, the social history, discovering times past, remembering the people who once lived their lives along the line, the events and places the railway affected, but she won't be persuaded. Jake enjoyed it though, especially the hunt for railway treasures. Archaeology, of all sorts, has to be *touched* to be believed.

The railway line began to curve slowly left and I realised we were heading back to the main road again. I could see some houses ahead. Beside a bridge, someone had roped off part of the line and made it into a children's football pitch, with the goal posts beneath the arch of the bridge. It was very neatly done.

Past the bridge, we came to Troutbeck station, still intact and in very good condition. A notice said 'Private', so it was obviously well and truly inhabited. I approached it from the fields, eventually getting over onto a fine platform and then reached a signal-box, the best one I'd seen so far. The upstairs part was still intact, and in good repair. I couldn't get into it as the ladder had gone, but I could see the levers and wires and rods. As I was wandering round, deciding whether I should climb into the signal-box, a car arrived at the neatly laid-out station garden, and an elderly couple got out. I immediately went towards them. There's one rule when trespassing, or when you fear you might be trespassing: apologise first. I explained what I was doing, that I was a Railway Rambler, with a badge to prove it, and after some hesitation, the gentleman invited me in.

He was called Gordon Carter and he not only lives in a converted station, he's still a railway worker, a booking clerk at Penrith station. It was nice to find someone who must know, and presumably love, the line as a professional.

He has worked on the line since 1935, when he joined as a junior porter at Bass Lake station. His stepfather before him worked for the C.K. and P. at Bass Lake, where his mother now lives in a railway cottage. He used the initials so smoothly, like a household word, so I might as well use them this time. On the closure of the line, in 1972, he had been one of the railway staff sent from Penrith to go down the line and look at all the stations and railway buildings and itemise what could be saved or sent to be sold at Collector's Corner in London.

Local councils, when a line closes, generally have first offer of the land and the buildings, but he got the chance to buy the station himself in 1976. He'd already been living in it for two years, so he knew all about it. He wouldn't reveal how much he paid for it. Knowing the BR Property Board, it probably wasn't a snip.

He seemed very matter-of-fact about living in an old station, unlike the engraver on the Aberdeen line, more concerned about possible changes in National Park laws that might affect him, rather than being swept away by the railwayanic romance of it all.

'I get enough at work with those nutters who run up and down the station with tape recorders. Terrible. They're never off your back. You should see all the fancy cameras they have these days. You wouldn't catch me walking the old line.'

However, he is nostalgic enough to have kept a few odd bits and pieces from the old days on the line, when he was a boy before the war, such as some C.K. and P. remittances and pay slips. But alas he couldn't find them. Next time I passed, he said, I must pop in and he would dig them out for me to see.

Before the railway finally reaches Penrith, it takes a very strange-looking loop to the north, curling sharply away from the road (both the new trunk road and the old B road), meandering round for about four miles when it could have got to Penrith in half the distance by carrying straight on. Perhaps it was trying to ease the gradients by curving round the contours.

There was a station at the furthest point of the loop, Blencow station, but even this was in the middle of nowhere as the village of Blencow is a good mile further on. Perhaps there was some large and important landowner on the direct route to Penrith who refused to sell his land. More probably, the railway made a deliberate detour to link up with the quarries around Newbiggin and was able to attract extra freight traffic.

It was a relief anyway to have crossed the trunk road and to wander into the hinterland on the other side of the Penrith plain. It seemed a different world, overgrown and hidden, private and mysterious. Crows screamed out at my presence as I crashed through the foliage, warning the wild life that an intruder was approaching.

I came to a little railwayman's hut, the usual sort of single room with a brick fireplace and the chimney-breast which you see everywhere on old railways, usually in terrible condition, often a dumping ground for dead sheep. This one had a fitted yellow carpet, a couch and a chair. The inside walls had been whitewashed and it looked at first sight very cosy and inviting, though I realised on inspection that it had been abandoned. Some time recently someone had made it a temporary home or hiding place, perhaps a tramp, a squatter, illicit lovers or an escaped convict. Not far away I could see what looked like a working quarry, with a factory building and recent debris, so it wouldn't have taken long for the hide-out to be detected, though even in built-up areas old railway lines are often completely ignored and forgotten by locals.

Further on I came to some more quarry works, a monster grave which suddenly opened up beside me, as if trying to swallow the old railway line. I looked down and saw, about fifty feet below, dozens of rabbits cavorting and bustling, running in and out of holes. I felt like a spy, catching them going through their secret games and rituals.

I found a tall railway signal with handles and wires still in position and the remains of light fittings, but I couldn't see any part worth taking, I mean examining for their railway history. I then found myself in a deep rock cutting with trees and bushes grown right across, turning it into a wooded tunnel. The hawthorn was in full bloom and so were the wild roses. I felt completely cut off from civilisation, till I almost fell over a large white object which turned out to be a Hoovermatic washing machine.

Blencow station was in surprisingly good order, renovated

and developed and turned into a modern house. I had felt sure from the map it would have gone by now. Outside the back door was a yellow British Rail van, so perhaps a railway worker still lived there. I knocked but no one answered.

There were further quarries, still in working order, and some modern works, Blencow Lime Quarries, with mountains of bricks and concrete slabs piled up nearby. It was strange to see all these signs of modern industry in such a comparative backwater. It prepared me for the shock once more of hitting the main route, and the awful trunk road into Penrith.

The Keswick railway joined the main line just south of Penrith, so it didn't have its own station in Penrith, just a platform where the little local train would wait if the big main-line train, coming up from London, heading for Carlisle and Scotland, was late. In the final days they couldn't afford to miss even a handful of passengers who wanted to transfer to the branch line.

Penrith station is still in use but of course no one changes trains at Penrith any more. Many of the main-line expresses don't even stop. The APT (Advanced Passenger Train) from London to Glasgow will probably in future not even stop at Carlisle either, rushing completely past the Lakes in a mad 125 mph panic, unaware of all the little trains that once ran right through the heart of Lakeland.

6 🚂 The Wirral Way

MERSEYSIDE'S LITTLE MIRACLE,
BUT WHATEVER HAPPENED TO
THE SANDS OF DEE?

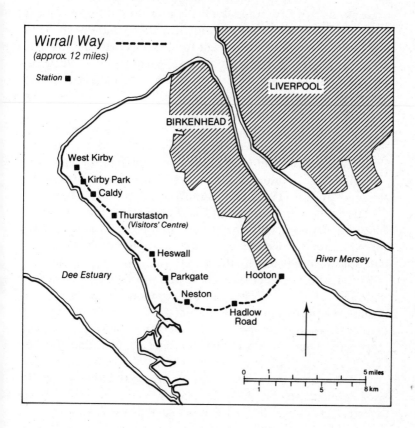

THE WIRRAL WAY is the showpiece of converted railways, a carefully created and smoothly running Rolls-Royce version of what an old railway can look like. It makes most local councils very envious, wishing they could turn their abandoned, rubbish-strewn lines into such beautiful works of art. And artifice. Some railway purists might think the Wirral Way is a little bit too organised, but after all, it is an official creation, deliberately designed to give pleasure to the 1½ million Merseysiders who live within a twelve-mile radius.

The Countryside Commission had great plans to have such converted railways all over the country, grant-aided under the Countryside Act. The Wirral Way was fortunately in at the beginning and became one of the first two country parks in the whole of Britain. The Commission's wonderful ideas began in the late 1960s, when money and aspirations were flowing freely. Cheshire County Council first took an interest in 1967, taking over the line in 1969, though there were many trials and tribulations before it was finally and formally opened in 1973 by Lord Leverhulme, to great acclaim and subsequent popularity.

Today, local councils haven't got any money to spare, thanks to all the Government's economic cut-backs, nor do they appear to have much interest in providing such marvellous educational and recreational facilities. The thousands of abandoned miles of old railways, all over the country, will probably rot for another decade, even those vast stretches already owned by local councils. In the places I visited where councils did have formal plans to use their local lines, such as Cockermouth and Keswick, the big problem was whether the money would ever be available to do the job properly.

The Wirral line closed to passengers in 1956 and had had a decade of neglect before the council bulldozers eventually moved in. 'The line was derelict,' says their Information Sheet. 'Much of it was a tip and refuge for vermin and a rendezvous for illicit love making in various forms.' Tut, tut. Whatever can that mean? How many forms of illicit love making are there? I've heard stories about those Liverpool scouses and their strange habits but surely the good county folk of Cheshire don't indulge in such things?

The line is twelve miles long, stretching from West Kirby, which is now part of the Metropolitan Borough of Wirral, along the Dee estuary to Hooton in Cheshire. (The two councils jointly run the line and pay its costs.) The Wirral Country Park, to give it its proper title, also includes several other pieces of land which connect with the original railway route, giving the public another fifteen miles of footpaths and bridleways. It means you can plan round walks, without having to come back the same way, with easy access to several places of interest up and down the line. There's a staff of six full-time Country Park Rangers and six part-time Rangers, to keep an eye on it, and you, plus another ten staff, from information assistants to cleaners.

Buying the basic twelve-mile stretch of line cost £98,000, a lot of money in 1969, but much of it did have building potential and BR always tries to get the best possible price. The total cost, so far, of acquiring and developing the line, including building the large and splendid Visitor Centre, is £350,000. The annual running costs are around £100,000. That all seems cheap to me, when you think it is available for those 1½ million Merseysiders.

So much for the facts. The flavour, well, that's much harder to pass on. I had read and heard a lot about it but it wasn't till I visited the line that I really appreciated its uniqueness.

You have firstly to look at a map to understand its situation, that's if, like me, you're not quite sure about the local Liverpool geography. I have visited Liverpool many times over the years and have even been to the Wirral, but I can't remember how I got there. I got confused by all the bits of water and complicated tunnels.

The Wirral is a peninsula, a wedge-shaped lump of land, which juts out into the Irish Sea. On its right side there's the relatively narrow Mersey estuary and on the left the much broader Dee estuary. I had realised that people who lived 'over the water', as they say in Liverpool, were the posh folk, the

Cheshire county types, but it's only when you stand on the Wirral peninsula that you can see and smell and feel the two cultures. Along the right-hand side of the Wirral, the view is pure Merseyside, a mass of industrial dockland, cranes and factories and skyscrapers dominating the landscape. On the left-hand side, just four miles away, it's another world, a peaceful, timeless estuary, green fields running down to undisturbed beaches and marshes, with beyond the beautiful coastline of North Wales. The old railway line is down this left side. No wonder they went to such trouble to save it. Liverpool desperately needed that lung.

Most aspects of life on the Wirral Way, past and present, have been meticulously charted. They have pamphlets and news-sheets, guides and charts for almost everything to do with the Walk. The Wirral Country Park Teacher's Pack alone contains 235 pages (a bargain at £3.75). Then there are audio-visual displays, relief maps, slide shows, films, show cases, flashing lights. I felt overwhelmed by all the information available, far more than I would ever wish to know, at least that's how it felt, coming straight from Cumbria and my failure to find even one booklet or information sheet devoted to the poor old Keswick line.

I started at the Visitor Centre which is where most of the Park's estimated half-million people a year start, and many never get much further. It's at Thurstaston, about two miles down the coast from West Kirby, a little complex of tastefully designed buildings, hidden by trees and little bridges and pretty ponds, on the site of the old Thurstaston station. The platforms are still there, and the line itself is very clear, but the original railway buildings have gone. (In fact there's only one station left on the line; the other eight were vandalised beyond recall.) The Visitor Centre is surrounded by grass, which stretches the few hundred yards or so to the sea, and it's all so well kept and trim that I had the impression of being on a very high-class golf course.

There is a camping site, but it is carefully hidden away, with room for sixty pitches and its own warden, as well as facilities for fishing, horse riding, nature trailing, bird watching, caravanning and having picnics. It reminded me very much of a holiday I once had in the Shenandoah National Park in the Blue Ridge Mountains of Virginia. It was the Americans, after all, who gave the idea of National Parks to the world, building their first in 1872, almost a hundred years before Britain got round to the idea.

At Shenandoah they have film screens, deep in the heart of what looks like virgin forest; trees which turn out to have light sockets fitted in the trunks; rocks with hidden buttons which when pressed give you a refreshing drink of ice cold water. Wonderful, but not all that wild. The Wirral planners went across to America to look at their National Parks, when setting up the Wirral Way, but fortunately, or unfortunately, depending on your point of view, they haven't copied all the American dreams.

Eric Jarvis is the Senior Ranger and was in charge the day I called. They were waiting to appoint a new Head Ranger. He's a tall, suitably rangy man of fifty-three and arrived in 1970 when the railway was just being reclaimed and cleaned up and fifty miles of new fences were being erected to rope off their verminous, sin-infested rendezvous. He comes from Gloucestershire and previously ran a turkey farm. They were looking, in those early days, when hiring their first Rangers, for mature chaps over thirty-five, preferably with an agricultural background. Over 170 people applied when, like Mr Jarvis, they saw the job advertised in the farming press. Today, a decade later, they usually go for younger men, and they can have up to 500 applicants whenever a Ranger's job is advertised.

Mr Jarvis's wife also works for the Park and is one of the information officers at the Visitor Centre. Like her husband, she is dressed in a green uniform, though he doesn't like the outfits to be described as a uniform. 'Distinctive clothing' is what he prefers. All the Rangers wear green trousers, green jacket, green shirt, green wellies and a green hat with a badge which is turned up at the side and makes them look like a cross between a stage Australian and a Tyrolean yodeller. The young Rangers usually manage not to wear their hats. Eric quite likes his.

Contractors are brought in for any heavy or large-scale work, such as reclaiming new land. (Through the will of an old lady they had just acquired some more fields near Caldy.) Contractors are also used for landscaping a rubbish dump, another job currently in hand, or for rebuilding sea walls, a job that regularly has to be done. Apart from that, all the day-to-day repairs are done by the Rangers themselves.

They pride themselves on the speed at which they make good the work of vandals – two notice boards had just been wrecked – or manage to pick up any litter by dusk each day, when the trippers have gone home. During the day I spent with Mr Jarvis he was perpetually bending over to pick up crisp packets and sweet papers, still talking away, his body not realising what it was doing, so ingrained has the clearing-up habit become.

All the Rangers have walkie-talkie radios strapped to their belts, which crackle away all day, keeping them in touch, sending messages down the line, warnings of crisp-eating vandals approaching. There are various by-laws they have to enforce, such as guns not being allowed, or cycling, though you can *push* your bicycle.

In the early years, when they were building all the new fences, local residents couldn't wait to be cut off from the dirty, old, vandalised railway line, very concerned that the new park might bring in even more hooligans. Now, as in every official council-run railway walk I visited, there are local residents who want to be *connected* to the railway once again, desperate to have their own little private garden gate on to the line. The Wirral Rangers have coped with the crowds, and the countryside, so successfully that there is talk of increasing their number and giving them jurisdiction over other nearby council common land.

The Wirral Way is open seven days a week, all round the year, and one Ranger is always on night patrol. They can't really shut it up, as it's an open park, but the lavatories and other buildings, plus the car parks, are closed every night.

The Visitor Centre is near the sea so I went to have my first look at the Dee Estuary and the Welsh coast, noticing on the way that even the litter bins round the Centre were painted green, with green plastic bags inside. The actual coast was a lovely surprise. I expected the grass to run straight into the sea but I suddenly came to a cliff, and below it a huge sandy coastal strip, with wader birds at rest and little sailing boats bobbing far out in the estuary. It was a *real* seaside. I'd half feared it might be little more than a muddy estuary.

Mr Jarvis gave me a lift to the beginning of the line, at Caldy near West Kirby, and left me to make my way back, arranging to meet me later. He told me to look out for the big houses where they'd sold off bits of their huge gardens for new developments. Even these new houses, inside the old gardens, seemed to have large gardens.

Many of Liverpool's powerful shipping magnates had their homes in this part of the Wirral, such as Sir Thomas Ismay, head of the White Star line. In the old days, between the wars, there used to be a queue of private horse-drawn coaches waiting at all the little stations along the line. The London and North Western Railway, who ran the line jointly with the GWR, had first-, second- and third-class coaches, as all trains did at one time, but they considered that this little branch line, because of all the important Liverpool businessmen who used it, deserved something even better than a first-class compartment. They therefore used to attach a 'Club' carriage to the train, a special LNW coach which had been fitted with armchair seats and bridge tables.

The population of the Wirral in 1866, when the first part of the branch line was completed (from Parkgate to Hooton), was rather sparse, with isolated farming communities, though there was coal-mining at Neston and on the coast itself there was a string of thriving little fishing ports, embarkation points for Ireland. The arrival of the railway opened up the countryside for commuters and gave better, speedier markets for the farmers and the fishermen. Throughout the summer, the trains were packed with Liverpool day trippers heading for seaside places like Parkgate.

I started at Caldy, where the station site is now a car park, and looking down along the coast I could see a sailing club, with trim little yachts moored out in the mud flats, waiting for the tide and the weekend sailors. Beside the line itself is a golf club, another sign of suburban man.

The track was straight and flat and very prettily overgrown with yellow gorse bushes in full bloom, white hawthorns and some very dark red wild roses. The old railway line has been

[97]

separated into two paths, one for horses and one for pedestrians, which go side by side almost the whole twelve miles. I didn't actually see any sailors, or golfers, horsemen or even walkers along this first stretch, all the way from Caldy to Thurstaston, despite the sunny day. I did see some very white-looking dog droppings, the sign of well-fed suburban dogs on their evening strolls.

This northern end of the line was added in 1886 and most of the bridges were built of purple brick. On the southern stretch, they're in sandstone. Local farmers, who had great power in the early days, deciding whether or not to sell out to the railways, could sometimes dictate their local railway architecture. There's one bridge in the purple brick section, just outside Parkgate, where the bridge is red because that was the colour the farmer desired. Really powerful landowners, like Thomas Ismay, could refuse all inducements. He made the railway detour round his property near Thurstaston, pushing it further on to the coast, which today, for walkers, gives an added pleasure. It was the first of my railway walks where I could actually do any walking beside the sea, though near Keswick I did have the gentle waves of Bassenthwaite.

I passed a rubbish dump on the right, which I'd been told, very apologetically, by the Senior Ranger, should really be ignored. It was nothing to be ashamed of as they've managed to get grass to grow over most of it, though it's rather wiry grass with old bottles and cans peeping through in places. They'd obviously had some bad luck with introducing young trees and shrubs. All that remained of many of them were the black plastic bags they'd been sheltering in over the winter, trying in vain to resist the strong, salt-laden winds which can ravage any tender vegetation along the Dee estuary.

When I reached Thurstaston again, a new load of children were rushing round the Visitor Centre, eating crisps. I asked one of them if he'd been on the old railway yet. 'Where's dat?' I pointed it out, but he didn't seem interested. The best part of the day, so he said, was crossing the Mersey on the ferry.

The Wirral Way breaks slightly at Heswall and you have to join a road for a short distance. Heswall station has gone but some railway cottages remain. There was a passing loop at

Heswall station, where trains could pass or overtake each other, but a driver could only enter the single track when he had been given a staff by the section signalman.

Heswall is one of the more desirable suburbs of the Wirral. Paul McCartney still has a house there, and you can't get more desirable than that. It was the final home of his delightful father Jim and I visited him there several times, before I understood the geography of the Wirral. His brother Michael McCartney, known professionally as Michael McGear on his records and TV appearances, still lives in Heswall, within spitting distance of the Wirral Way.

'I watch the hikers every Sunday,' said Michael. 'There's millions of them. It's one of my favourite places for a walk with my children, but we always go mid-week to avoid the crowds.

'I used to love steam railways as a kid. Me and Paul used to play dangerous games on the main line, watching the trains going into Liverpool towards Lime Street. They had open engines in those days and we used to shout at the drivers on the footplate. The game was to see what they would shout back. I love old-fashioned steam railways. Much better than the new stuff. I don't think much of them at all.'

However, despite living on the Wirral Way, he'd never walked the full distance, and wasn't even aware that it had all been laid out as a proper path. This I had found several times already on my railway walks – that local people were not aware of what had been done on their doorsteps. Before I left Heswall, I got him to promise that he'd go the full distance with his children very soon.

At Parkgate I finally came face to face with the great mystery of the Dee estuary. From the sixteenth century, Parkgate was a flourishing town and sea port, with the packet boats going straight across to Ireland. When the railway arrived, their cockles and mussels were able to be transported direct to Liverpool, Manchester and London. It still is very much a seaside town, with a very handsome sea front, full of old fishermen's houses, ancient inns, merchants' dwellings. The little fish shops still advertise fresh shrimps, even boasting they've been caught locally. It's only when you turn your back on the harbour front, perhaps sit on the old stone mooring posts, and look out to sea, that you begin to feel disorientated. Instead of ships bobbing up and down in the harbour, there stretches before you over half a mile of shimmering grass.

Parkgate's rise to seaside fame started when it replaced Chester which between the eleventh and fourteenth centuries was the major port on the whole north-western coast. The Dee estuary was then twenty miles long and about five miles wide. By the sixteenth century, when Parkgate took over, the shifting sands had begun to silt up the port of Chester, eventually leaving it high and dry. Today, the Dee estuary is about half the size and Chester is around ten miles away from any sea, and about three hundred years away from its maritime past.

The silting up of Parkgate has happened within living memory. People can remember just fifty years ago when boats moored at Parkgate. Now it is only perhaps once or twice a year, on exceptional spring tides, that any sea water crawls over the grass and marsh and reaches the old harbour.

Beside the old railway line you can see the remains of Parkgate's open-air baths. The walls are still in place, enclosing two pools which the sea filled and washed clean at each high tide. They were built in 1923 by A. G. Grenfell of Mostyn House School, which still stands on the front at Parkgate. Adults paid one shilling and juveniles sixpence which seems a lot but the swimming was highly fashionable and reputedly very healthy and for a time Parkgate was known as Deauville en Wirral. The silting of the Dee caused the baths to be closed in 1942. I peered behind the walls of the old pool and saw only grass and shrubs, then a quick movement as a courting couple made themselves respectable.

Parkgate has an interesting history. Almost every building has a maritime connection and was visited or lived in by many famous people, all carefully detailed in an excellent little booklet on sale at the Visitor Centre. Sir Wilfred Grenfell, the great explorer, was born in Parkgate, the brother of A. G. Grenfell of Mostyn House School. He became nationally famous in 1908 after the publication of his autobiography, *A Labrador Doctor*. It described how he was crossing the frozen waters of Newfoundland by sledge, on the way to a patient, when the ice began to break up. He survived the night by killing his three huskies and wrapping himself in their skins. In the Mostyn House chapel he placed a memorial tablet: 'In grateful memory of my rescue from a drifting iceflow and of three brave dogs, Moody, Watch and Spy, whose lives were sacrificed to save mine.'

Lady Hamilton, when she was plain Emma Lyon, not yet a lady, nor Admiral Nelson's mistress, came for a holiday in Parkgate in 1784 with her mother, attracted by reports of the excellent sea bathing which she thought might improve a skin complaint. 'The price is high,' so she wrote in a letter about her lodging house in what is now Station Road Cottage, 'but it is comfortable, decent and quiet and I thought it would not ruin us. The sea watter has done me so much good. I have drunk a tumbler glas every morning fasting, walked half an hour, then bathed and breakfasted. I am oblidged to give a shilling a day for the bathing horse and whoman and twopence a day for the dress. It is a great expense, and it frets me when I think of it. I have the tang [seaweed] applyed to my kne and elbows every night going to bed and every day washed them twice a day in the sea water and they are just as well.'

Mrs Fitzherbert, the lady friend of George IV, was also a visitor to Parkgate, staying at the Talbot Inn around 1798. Perhaps Cheshire has always had an attraction for ladies of a certain reputation, even before the railway's illicit pleasure-seekers.

Probably the most famous visitor to Parkgate was Handel. I had been told that Handel had written the *Water Music* in Parkgate, while waiting to get a boat to Dublin, which would have been a nice memento of its maritime past. The Parkgate and District Society's little booklet says that it was the *Messiah* which would have been in Handel's head, as he was on his way to its first performance in Dublin, and that he stayed in Chester, not Parkgate. He had intended to sail from Parkgate, but the winds were wrong, though he did visit Parkgate on his way back from Ireland in August 1742.

The big attraction of Parkgate today, apart from the handsome houses and the many quaint inns, still very popular with evening visitors from Liverpool, is the bird life. You often see long lines of amateur ornithologists, staring through their binoculars, right along the old sea walls near Parkgate, studying the grasses, marshes and mud flats. When the tide comes near, it disturbs the millions of little animals and insects which live on the marsh lands, and down swoop the birds.

The mud flats on the estuary are twice as rich in organic life as a comparable stretch of good agricultural land, and fifty times richer than the open ocean. The cockles have mostly gone, but the shrimps jump on and so do many other forms of sea life. Kestrels are common, as are sparrow-hawks and short-eared owls, ready to dive on any likely food silly enough to move. Waders have been estimated in flocks of up to 100,000. Seals are often seen, and so are dolphins, porpoises and even killer whales. Above all, the Dee estuary is renowned as being a home of one of Britain's rarest amphibians, the natterjack toad.

Despite having read the Wirral Way booklets, I'm still not quite sure why the Dee silted up so quickly and so dramatically. The Mersey estuary, by comparison, has hardly changed, but no doubt they keep that clear with modern dredgers. The Dee estuary does have strange tides and it was always very shallow anyway. Perhaps the Mersey, being narrower, keeps the water flowing more quickly. No doubt there are geological and physical explanations somewhere which I've failed to find.

All the same, I can see why so many people now want to save the silted-up estuary, to stop any threat of its being made into a reservoir or converted for agriculture or factories. It is a perfect wild-life sanctuary. And as for railway walkers, the estuary is a wonderful alternative to coming back along the line you've just explored.

The next excitement on the Wirral Way, judging by the amount of leaflets and explanatory notes, is the rock cutting at Neston. This is a dramatic quarter-mile stretch which has been dynamited through solid sandstone. The rock sides reach about twenty-five feet high in parts, mostly now a mass of tree roots, mosses, lichens and other forms of jungle-like vegetation, especially on the southern side, the wettest part. It's like a deep green cavern, always damp and dark and mysterious, even on the sunniest summer day. In the railway days, it used to echo to the sounds of cursing loco men and shrieking brakes as their engines often slipped on the wet and slimy rails.

As you approach from the Neston end, there's a monster

growth down the middle, like a giant ocean centipede which has been left stranded by some long-forgotten Deeside flood. It turns out to be a sewage pipe which was put in by the local council when the line first closed, intending eventually to fill in the whole cutting. It's now been carefully allowed to be over-grown with the same sort of mosses, grasses and plant life which have taken over the rocks' sides. Very soon, it will be impossible to tell that the pipe was man-made.

When the line was being cleared, back in 1970, to open it to the public, they took out twenty lorry-loads of junk which had been tipped over the sides. Even now, they take out a lorry-load a year of people's refuse. This, of course, is the fate of any deep and empty railway cutting. It's so easy to back your car towards it in the evening, chuck out the rubbish, and then get away without being seen. Only the foxes down below, disturbed in their lairs, or the wrens, which love to nest in the cuttings, will know what has happened.

There's a nature trail guide for the cutting which tells child-ren, or anyone else, how to look out for and recognise the strange shell creatures, the beetles, centipedes and woodlice which live in the cutting. On one visit, so the guide maintains, you could spot seven sorts of grasses, sixteen types of herbs, five sorts of trees and shrubs, four ferns, four mosses, two liverworts, two lichens, and associated algae in the puddles.

Just to finish off the facts, the whole twelve miles of the Wirral Way has been religiously examined for its flora and fauna, and according to the teachers' pack it is possible to identify 114 different species of birds and 120 sorts of wild flowers.

On the left-hand side of the cutting there are two dates to be seen. One of them, carved in the sandstone, says 1866, the year the cutting was created. The other says 1964, the year the track was finally taken up, perhaps inscribed by one of the contrac-tor's workmen, idling away his lunch break.

The final glory of the Wirral Way, and one not to be missed, even on a fleeting visit, is the station at Hadlow Road, the only surviving station on the line.

I thought at first I was suffering from an optical illusion. On my walks so far I had become used to deserted stations, peering through broken glass, looking for cracks in boarded-up doors, climbing through crumbling walls, kicking a way over the debris, or alternatively admiring what some proud householder had done to convert his old railway property into a modern home. On this occasion, I found myself suddenly face to face with what looked like a *real* station. The platforms were neat and tidy, the iron rails gleaming, and some milk trolleys were waiting to be loaded on the next train. On the station walls were adverts for Bovril, Brooke Bond Tea, Hudson's Super Soap, Hignets Smoking Mixture, 4d per oz.

I went inside and the booking office was also in perfect condition, the phone off the hook as if the station-master had just popped out to pass on a message to the porter or signalman. The kettle was on the hob, the tickets neatly arranged, the lamps cleaned, the timetables open, railway weighing scales ready, the railwaymen's caps on the pegs. It was all exactly as it must have been in the 1950s, down to the correct posters and furniture. It was a rather eerie experience.

Hadlow Road station has to be called a replica station, though that's not strictly correct as it is a *real* station, with *real* fittings. Cheshire County Council, when they took over the line, decided to preserve the station as it had recently been. Some of the equipment came from elsewhere but there are photographs of the station staff who used to work there.

The only jarring note, and for a moment I thought it too might be genuine, is a notice announcing that this is a local agency for Wells Fargo and Express. That's one of the Rangers' jokes. They found the tin notice when cleaning out a local rubbish dump and hung it in the station, just to see if the railway experts would spot it.

The station is un-manned, un-curated, un-guarded, which is something of a miracle. A cleaner opens it each morning, then it's left for anyone to wander in and wander round. The rest of the station is lived in by a Ranger, but it's not his job to guard the little railway museum. Liverpool, as most locals will tell you, suffers from heavy vandalism, and even cars parked in the streets are not considered safe. Yet Hadlow Road station has never been vandalised. I only hope mentioning such a commendable state of affairs won't encourage anyone to spoil its record.

I walked back to the Visitor Centre at Thurstaston, where

I'd parked my car, and enjoyed the walk just as much as I'd
done on the way there. I walked this time as much as possible
along the estuary. I tried hard in the evening gloom to hear any
ghostly voices calling the cattle home across the sands towards
Wales, my next stop on my railway walks, but I heard nothing.

My mother used to recite that poem by Charles Kingsley to
me when I was little, about poor Mary getting lost on the Sands
of Dee. It's probably the best-known of those maudlin Victorian
ballads, guaranteed to bring out the tears. At the time, I
imagined it was a Scottish poem, referring to the Aberdeen
river Dee. When you actually see the sands of this river Dee, as
Kingsley saw them over a hundred years ago, you can clearly
understand how easy it must have been to be cut off as the Dee
plays yet another of its tricks.

> *O Mary, go and call the cattle home,*
> *And call the cattle home,*
> *And call the cattle home,*
> *Across the sands of Dee;*
> *The Western wind was wild, and dank with foam,*
> *And all alone went she.*
>
> *The Western tide crept up along the sand,*
> *And o'er and o'er the sand,*
> *And round and round the sand,*
> *As far as the eye could see.*
> *The rolling mist came down and hid the land:*
> *And never home came she.*
>
> *Oh! is it weed, or fish, or floating hair –*
> *A tress of golden hair,*
> *A drowned maiden's hair*
> *Above the nets at sea?*
> *Was never salmon yet that shone so fair*
> *Among the stakes on Dee.*
>
> *They rowed her in across the rolling foam,*
> *The cruel crawling foam,*
> *The cruel hungry foam,*
> *To her grave beside the sea;*
> *But still the boatmen hear her call the cattle home*
> *Across the sands of Dee.*

7 The Wye Valley

WALKING WITH OFFA, WORDSWORTH AND SOME OLD WELSH RAILWAY WORKERS

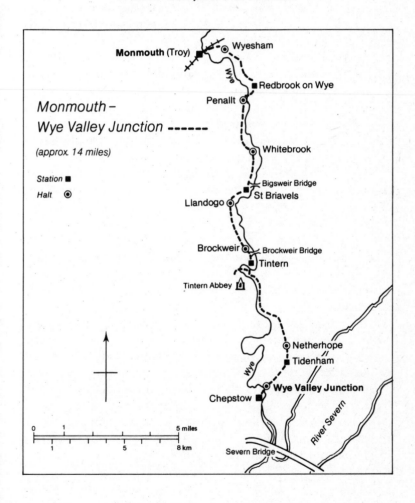

Monmouth –
Wye Valley Junction ------

(approx. 14 miles)

Station ■

Halt ◉

Monmouth (Troy)
Wyesham
Wye
Redbrook on Wye
Penallt
Whitebrook
Bigsweir Bridge
St Briavels
Llandogo
Brockweir
Brockweir Bridge
Tintern
Tintern Abbey
Netherhope
Tidenham
Wye
Wye Valley Junction
Chepstow
River Severn
Severn Bridge

0 1 5 miles
1 5 8 km

THE LOWER WYE VALLEY is in the south-east of Wales, right on the borders of Wales and England. It's a deep, wooded, meandering valley which runs south into the Severn estuary. Such facts are easy to trot out. When it comes to describing its *riches*, it is much harder to know where to begin.

The Wye is rich in beauty, for a start, which is why it has been designated an Area of Outstanding Natural Beauty. Local planners and officials persist in using the initials A.O.N.B. when talking or writing about it which immediately takes away all its personality, making it sound like an army command. They initial it out of love and pride, of course, as they are pleased to have an officially designated area in their jurisdiction.

Then it's rich in history, from the Romans, through the Dark Ages to medieval and modern times. There's also a whole host of literary connections. The industrial past is equally fascinating. One is so bombarded, the minute one enters the valley, by the Wales Tourist Board or Gwent County Council, the Ramblers' Association and other bodies, describing the mouth-watering walks to be had, industrial archaeology to be explored, castles and abbeys to be visited, that at first it all seems terribly confused.

There are three different trails to follow up the Wye valley, which cross each other from time to time, in past and present, each with its own identity. I really wanted only one, but it would be perverse to completely ignore the others.

So I sat down very quietly on a big stone near Chepstow and had some deep thoughts. I was right at the edge of the Severn estuary, on Sedbury Cliffs. Beneath me were the mud flats of the Severn, and then the wide surging waters of the estuary itself, and beyond in the far distance, Bristol and the West of England, whence I'd come that morning.

I'd been in London only two hours previously, which was an amazing thought. Until very recently, it took the best part of a day to get from London to this corner of South Wales. Thanks to the BR's wonderful Inter-City 125 train, I'd got to Bristol Parkway from Paddington in just one hour, eleven minutes. Then I'd hired a car to drive myself to Chepstow which took a little over fifteen minutes, all thanks of course to the even more wonderful Severn Bridge, opened by the Queen in 1966. The ancients, those people who lived in the dark days of the 1950s, would not believe such progress.

The large block of sandstone I was sitting on had the word 'Mods' daubed on it in white paint, a piece of 1960s graffiti. It marks the beginning of Offa's Dyke. Or the end, depending on which way you start. Either way, the Wye valley offers you a 170-mile-long public footpath, from Chepstow right across the edge of Wales to Prestatyn on the Irish Sea, following for the most part the route which Offa laid down.

The Dyke is the most unusual of Britain's long-distance footpaths, officially opened in 1971. It is unique as a walk in that if follows a man-made monument, not a natural line, such as a coast or range of hills, like the Cornish long-distance walk or the Pennine Way. Historically, it is the most interesting survival from the darkest of the Dark Ages.

The darkness fell after the Romans left, leaving the Anglo-Saxons to fight it out amongst themselves. The Romans had found conquering and controlling Wales troublesome enough and they established two great fortresses, at Caerleon and Chester, and for a long time based two legions in Wales. The Romans were the first to define the border land between Wales and the rest of England.

Offa emerged as King of Mercia in 757 and for the next forty years established himself as the strongest Anglo-Saxon king, controlling most of England south of Yorkshire. He was treated as an equal by continental rulers such as Charlemagne with whom he signed a treaty. He married one of his daughters to the King of Wessex and another to the King of Northumbria and so created relative peace on those two flanks.

He'd had several great wars against the Welsh kingdoms and around 784, at a time of reasonable stability, decided to mark the western boundaries of his kingdom once and for all by building a dyke, as a political and economic boundary as much as a military defence. He utilised, where possible, natural features, such as hills and rivers. The Dyke itself, when finished, is thought to have run for eighty-one miles. It was a colossal earthern worm, about sixty feet across and around ten feet high, including a steep ditch on the Welsh or western side.

Those of us who have seen and walked Hadrian's Wall naturally consider that to be the superior construction, as it was built 650 years earlier and was made of stone and was a much bigger feat of engineering, containing many castles and fortresses. Nonetheless, having to shift all that earth and dig all those ditches in a wild and mountainous region, makes Offa's Dyke a tremendous undertaking.

The Dyke became a language barrier as well as a political frontier. Even today, you can see the linguistic divisions with Old English place-endings like 'ham' and 'ton' to the east of the Dyke and Welsh names like 'tre' and 'llan' to the west. Where the Dyke was never built, there are clear linguistic inroads either side.

I could quite clearly see the line of the Dyke, a raised wooded hedgerow going down and across the field ahead of me. Behind me was the highly modernistic Severn Road Bridge; two marvels of engineering, 1,200 years apart.

The bridge looked as if it had just fallen from the heavens, so huge and sky-size, dwarfing all other objects on the horizon, man-made or natural. Its two huge, 400-foot towers seemed to be supporting a giant's trapeze line with little insects buzzing over, defying all the elements by being suspended in mid-air. The insects were motor cars, doing 70 mph as I had done. With the right sort of rifle, I felt I could pick them off. Offa's revenge.

I set off for Chepstow, following the Dyke, and came to a stile and a yellow arrow and a white acorn – at least two blobs of white which I took to be an acorn design – marking the way. There were further arrows and acorns when I crossed a road, leading me into another field towards a council estate.

The directions are clear on Offa's Dyke all the way to North Wales and there are excellent maps and guide books available from the Ramblers' Association and from the Offa's Dyke Association – the latter publish sectional maps which include almost every field. There were no written signs on the little bit I walked into Chepstow, to tell me it was Offa's Dyke, but apparently, further on, some signs bear the names Offa's Dyke Path or Llwybr Clawdd Offa.

I did notice some nice street names on the way through the suburbs of Chepstow, such as Offa's Close, Mercian Way, Norse Way and King Alfred's Road, but I was mainly keeping an eye out for a first glimpse of Chepstow Castle, perched on the limestone cliffs above the Wye, built in the eleventh century by the Norman invader, William FitzOsborn.

The road bridge over the Wye, still the main entrance to the town, was built by John Rennie in 1816 and is one of the earliest cast-iron bridges in Britain. The railway bridge came later, being built by Brunel in 1852. The main span, over 300 feet long, was carried by two tubes, a revolutionary idea at the time. He got them into place by harnessing the exceptionally high tides on the Wye – a system used by the engineers in fitting sections of the modern Severn Bridge. Brunel's tubes were replaced when the bridge was reconstructed in 1962.

Chepstow, a very attractive town, with fine narrow medieval streets, is a good starting point for any of the three trails up the Wye valley. I was now about to temporarily leave the first one, Offa's Dyke, which keeps to the right of the town, on the other side of the river.

The second trail, equally well blazed and routed, is the Wye Valley Walk. It begins in Chepstow, and wanders close to the river some thirty-four miles up to Ross-on-Wye. The route is waymarked with yellow arrows and yellow dots, just so you don't get it mixed up with the yellow arrows for Offa's Dyke Path.

The third trail, alas, is not signposted at all, except where by chance, cutting back and forward across the river like a drunken sailor, it overlaps parts of Offa's Dyke and parts of the Wye Valley Walk. This is the trail I had come to follow, the one left by the Wye Valley Railway, now deceased.

In many ways the railway route is the best of them all, giving a taste of all worlds, all aspects of Wye valley life, past and present– if of course you can find it and then manage to follow it. When you consider how publicised the Wye valley is, how opened up for the tourists, it is strange how hard it is to get any information on the Wye Valley Railway Company, though

Gwent County Council were helpful in giving me out-of-print references and documents from their archives. I suppose the valley is walked enough and there is no need, nor the money, for the council to signal even more routes, but I would have thought some local railway society might have produced a guide-book to the line.

It was a single-track branch line, linking Chepstow with Monmouth. It began at a junction just one mile north of Chepstow, Wye Valley Junction, and followed the river thirteen miles upstream to join the existing GWR line at Monmouth. It was opened in 1876, well after the mad days of the railway age, so they should have known, economically, what they were doing by then. Four stations were built, at Tidenham, Tintern, Bigswein (later called St Briavels) and Redbrook, two tunnels, and two iron girder bridges, and the total cost was just over £300,000. Most of it went into the tunnels.

Great things were expected of the Wye Valley line and the opening ceremonies received national publicity (in the *Illustrated London News* of 28 October 1876) and locally in the *Monmouthshire Beacon*. 'Whilst opening up a new district hitherto unapproached by railway traffic, the new line will prove a great convenience not only to the locality through which it runs, but to the travelling public at large', so said the *Monmouthshire Beacon* of 21 October 1876.

There were representatives of the GWR at the opening ceremonies, plus directors of the Wye Valley Railway Company and local dignitaries. It was hoped that the line would revitalise some of the old industries of the Wye Valley, such as the tinplate works at Redbrook, paper mills at Whitebrook and the wire works, one of the oldest in the country, at Tintern. These wire works were set up in 1566, the first wire mills in Britain to use water power. A short branch line of the new railway was connected directly to the wire works. It was also hoped that the line would be of use to the traveller. For around a hundred years, the Wye valley had been a popular attraction for the country's better class of tourist.

The line did succeed in capturing the last of the commercial traffic, which until its opening was still using the river itself. In fact it killed off the river transport completely, but they miscalculated how large a trade that was going to be. In their estimate of annual revenue, which they were foolish enough to boast about at the time of their opening, they talked of annual receipts of £37,000. This was quickly proved to be wildly optimistic. Average receipts for the first ten years came to just over £5,000 a year. The ancient industries of the Wye valley, now of great fascination to industrial archaeologists, had had their day anyway and were moving elsewhere in South Wales or to the Midlands of England.

The wire-making works at Tintern turned to tin in the 1880s and then finally closed completely in 1901. There had always been some argument over the running and repair of the little works line, and the river bridge connecting it to the Wye Valley Railway. The railway company had never officially owned it, nor took an income, though they were expected to pay for its upkeep. The land was owned by the Duke of Beaufort, still a big landowner in this border region of Wales.

The GWR finally took over the Wye Valley line in 1905, though they had been involved with it from the beginning, providing the locomotives and working the line in return for half the receipts. In the 1920s and 1930s, several halts were added to the existing four stations – at Netherhope, Brockweir, Llandogo, Whitebrook, Penallt and Wyesham.

It was always a very scenic line, though very slow. The 14½-mile journey from Chepstow to Monmouth took just over fifty minutes, an average speed of seventeen miles an hour, not much more than the old horse coaches could do, though the trains did have all those stations and halts to stop at. By the 1950s it was losing an average of £13,000 a year. The end was nigh, even before Dr Beeching. It closed to passengers in 1959 and to goods in 1964.

The last passenger trip on the Wye Valley Railway was on Sunday 4 January 1959. Three hundred members of the Stephenson Locomotive Society (named after the loco, not the engineer) made the journey on a special train, from Chepstow to Ross-on-Wye. And so ended what was called by the railway press, reporting the last ride, 'the most beautiful journey in Britain'.

Most of the line was taken up following the final goods closure in January 1964, and sold for scrap, except for the first section, from Wye Valley Junction signal-box to Tintern Quarry, which is still used by BR as a mineral line. I therefore made my way to Tintern itself, to look for any railway remnants.

I got rather side-tracked in Tintern, as you might imagine. After all, in the Wye valley you can't ignore Offa, nor the famous abbey. I'd been looking out for it for some time, convinced from Wordsworth's poem that I would be able to see it from afar, dominating the landscape, but I failed to see it until I was almost upon it. The village of Tintern consists of a long strip of houses, bending in a large arc, following the deep bend of the river gorge. Because of the bends, Tintern Abbey can hardly be seen from the road until you reach it. Nonetheless, it was a fine sight.

The church itself, which is enormous, appears at first glance to be complete, as the walls are still at their original height; then you realise there is no roof and the glass from the long windows has all gone; a strange skeleton, the flesh stolen or rotted away, the original Romantic Ruine.

The abbey, which was built in the thirteenth century, was dissolved by Henry VIII in 1536, when he began to order all the monasteries to be closed, determined to realise their assets. The lead from the roof was melted down and the abbey was left to rot for around two-hundred years, with its owner, the Duke of Beaufort, taking little interest. Fashions changed in the late eighteenth century. Gothic architecture became suddenly fashionable again and gentlemen went on walking tours, specially to look at wild ruins like Tintern Abbey.

Guide books, such as the Rev. William Gilpin's in 1782, described how the abbey should be admired and viewed as a good example of the Picturesque, though he personally thought a little demolition might improve it. 'Though the parts are beautiful, the whole is ill shaped ... a number of gable ends hurt the eye with their regularity ... a mallet judiciously used (but who durst use?) might be of service in fractiring.'

Gilpin recommended sailing down the Wye to visit the abbey, using covered boat with plenty of hampers of food and drink supplied by the inkeepers in Ross or Monmouth, but he warned that there were some things that might upset gentlemen of refined tastes. Care must be taken 'so that the ear is not pained with coarseness of language too frequently heard from the navigators of public rivers'.

When Wordsworth and his sister Dorothy visited the abbey in 1798, they were simply trippers, part of the constant stream of visitors which was keeping the boat men occupied, the guides in business and beggars in regular crumbs. That same year, Turner visited Tintern, one of several visits he made, and produced his well-known water-colours of the abbey.

It was Wordsworth's second trip. He had visited the abbey alone some five years previously, as he describes in his poem, 'Lines Written a Few Miles Above Tintern Abbey on Revisiting the Banks of the Wye during a Tour, July 13, 1798', to give it its full title. This time he walked up from Chepstow with his sister, then took a boat back, returning to Bristol three days later. His *Lyrical Ballads* was already at the printers but he wrote his Tintern poem in a sudden burst of inspiration and rushed it to the printers unaltered, which was unusual for him. He always looked back fondly on the writing of 'Tintern Abbey'. 'No poem of mine was composed under circumstances more pleasant for me to remember.' It became the last poem in *Lyrical Ballads*, and the best received, and can be considered the first poem of what became the Romantic movement.

The horrors of the French Revolution had still been in his mind when he'd previously visited the abbey in 1793, and he was in a most unsettled and turbulent state, but now five years later he was with his beloved sister and was able to look upon nature in a different light. 'For I have learnt to look upon nature, not as in the hour of thoughtless youth, but hearing oftentimes the still, sad music of humanity.'

Wordsworth doesn't actually describe the abbey in the poem, as it is the mysticism of nature which mainly concerns him, but it has made Tintern famous throughout the English-speaking world.

They have an excellent exhibition area at the abbey in which they make a lot of the Wordsworth connection. I noticed a little pine-wood table, with a couple of smooth plastic chairs, and a sign above saying 'Info-Bar', all very modern and polished like a coffee bar, or perhaps a hamburger haven. I put in 10p, as

directed, and half expected an arm to appear and pour me out
a cup of plastic coffee, but instead out came the sonorous tones
of John Snagge. Had the Boat Race moved to the river Wye?
I listened carefully and heard him reading 'The Fascinating
Story of Tintern Abbey,' complete with Welsh voices singing,
bells chiming and actors pretending to be medieval monks.

On the way out, past a notice saying *DIM YSMYGU, DIM
CWN* (no smoking, no dogs), I asked the man at the ticket
counter if the voice really was John Snagge, or had I imagined
it. Yes, said the man, who turned out to be Frank Kelly, the
abbey's custodian, it was indeed John Snagge but his voice was
soon to be faded out. The Info-Bar owners now thought Mr
Snagge was too lugubrious and they were going to change the
tape to another voice.

The abbey gets between 150,000 and 200,000 visitors a year,
said Mr Kelly. Before the Severn Bridge was built, they got only
60,000. Local life, since the Severn Bridge, has never been the
same again. House and land prices doubled almost overnight
as the Wye valley suddenly came within easy distance of daily
commuters working in Bristol and weekenders from London.
Tintern itself now has many commercial travellers living in the
village. Since the bridge and the M4, it has become a perfect
place for them to live, within easy motoring reach of London,
Birmingham and South Wales. 'I know a local bungalow that's
just sold for £65,000. When I came here in 1967 it cost £8,000.
Prices have gone mad. The whole Wye valley has had the most
enormous tourist boom, though a lot of the locals don't like it.
They've been reluctantly dragged into the twentieth century.'

Mr Kelly used to be in the police force, before he retired as
a chief superintendent, having completed fourteen years as
personal bodyguard to Prince Philip. He kept a diary of those
years, and one day hopes to write it up as a book. He travelled
with Prince Philip to Antarctica and to South America where
they got mixed up in a revolution. He never had to make any
personal intervention of the sort which Prince Charles's bodyguard once had to make – when an intruder burst into Prince
Charles's bedroom and put his hands round the Prince's neck.
The bodyguard arrived in time and knocked him out cold,
which is what Mr Kelly says he would have done, had it been

Prince Philip. He has several pairs of cufflinks from his royal days, monogrammed **PP**, mementoes of stirring overseas journeys.

He knew nothing about Tintern Abbey when he got the job as custodian in 1967, but has done a lot of reading since about its history. He has a staff of two but still takes school parties round himself. 'I prefer a tidy group of children. It stops them climbing all over the walls.'

One of the commonest questions he gets asked is when was it bombed. An American once told him that if they had such a ruin in the States they'd put a Bubble over it to preserve it. 'I took a school party round the abbey once and on the way out a boy told me it was the nicest castle he'd ever visited.'

I then went through Tintern village and crossed the river by the little bridge, the one which formerly carried the little wagon way from the wire works to the Wye Valley Railway. The bridge is now owned by the council and is very popular with walkers, going to join the Offa's Dyke Path on the crest of the valley. I followed the old tracks where the works wagons used to run, looking directly across the river to the abbey, a better view of it than from the road.

I asked a man walking his dog where Tintern tunnel was, one of the two tunnels on the railway line itself. He said it was hard to find. It was probably blocked up by now, though he had walked through it some years ago. The track was overrun with bushes and trees, but if I looked out for the junction, then turned left along it, I should come to the entrance.

Tintern tunnel was open, when I eventually found it. The opening had indeed been blocked up with cement blocks but a narrow doorway had been left open, or perhaps broken open. I walked a few yards inside, expecting my senses to be hit by a sudden draught of soot and smoke, but there was hardly any. On previous railway tunnels I'd walked through, the smells still lingered on, decades after the last train had gone.

I was soon completely in the dark, the ballast sounding like thunder beneath my feet, echoing down the tunnel. It began to smell more like a railway tunnel, as I got further inside. I was about to turn back, partly out of fear but mainly because it seemed a pointless walk, when I suddenly saw a little spot of light ahead. I thought it might be a ventilation shaft but as I got nearer I realised it was the end. The tunnel makes a large curve and in the middle you can just see a pin-prick of light from either end, though at the ends themselves you can see only darkness.

I could hear water dripping as I approached the far end and I began to wonder if perhaps there had been a flood, or an avalanche, and I might get cut off. My eyes were more used to the gloom now and I could make out little alcoves cut in the rock at intervals along the tunnel.

I hastened my step slightly towards the end, but it was just as well I didn't proceed too quickly. I suddenly emerged into the daylight and found myself looking down at a sheer drop, straight over a cliff into the deep brown waters of the Wye below me. The railway bridge had long since been taken down and it was now a dead end. Across the river, if my map reading was correct, should be the site of the old Tintern railway station.

I worked my way back, counting 250 paces through the tunnel, just to take my mind off the dark, and returned to Tintern and then up the road towards the old station. It used to upset the villagers of Tintern that they had such a long walk to their local station. It was built some distance away, and was made to serve the next community of Brockweir as well, partly because of problems with local landlords and also because of the configuration of the river gorge which makes a large loop at Tintern.

Tintern station was a delightful surprise. I knew the building had been saved, because it is mentioned in the Wye Valley Walk leaflet, but I hadn't realised it had been retained as a railway station, with period signs, advertisements and furnishings, just like the one on the Wirral Way. Local councils can be imaginative, given a little encouragement and a bit of money.

It was completely derelict and vandalised, as was the signal-box opposite, when the council took it over in 1970, and had been empty for about ten years. A lot of the early site-clearing work was done by boys from an approved school in Chepstow. There's an exhibition in the main part of the station building, which includes before and after railway photographs, as well as a visual display of other aspects of Wye valley life.

The site warden, Ann Cooke, took me round and told me about the many awards the station has won, from Civic Trust awards to a Prince of Wales Award. I was suitably impressed and got out my camera, a brand-new Olympus Trip, given to me as a wedding anniverary present from my wife. So far, I'd been unable to work it, never having had a camera in my life before. But I thought such a lovely station called for some show of appreciation. I should really have had a camera when I began my first railway walks, just to look like a real railway enthusiast. You can't see the the true ones for lenses. I took some shots of the station, and the signal-box, quite prepared for them never to come out, and to celebrate Mrs Cooke made me some coffee in her little office in the signal-box. She's the wife of a local farmer and became site warden when the station was opened to the public in 1975. She wears a uniform of brown skirt, brown pullover and cream shirt and hands out lots of work sheets and information kits to school parties.

The site gets 40,000 visitors a year and she too has noticed a huge increase in the number and types of tourists since the Severn Bridge opened. She helps people find accommodation, camping sites, good walks, places of interest, the nearest garage. She'd recently had one family whose problem was that they didn't know where they were staying. They'd booked into a bed and breakfast place, left their belongings, but couldn't remember its name. 'All they could tell me was that they were staying near a castle.' As the valley is full of castles, that didn't help much, but eventually Mrs Cooke tracked it down.

The site also includes about half a mile of the old track, which today is neatly cared for and dotted with picnic tables. Mrs Cooke walked along her stretch with me as I headed on my way again. 'On the night Mafeking was relieved, the engine-driver stopped his train at Tintern station, rushed out to a pub to celebrate, leaving his whistle on. It ran dry and ruined his boiler. That's the story anyway.'

She apologised for a two-arm signal on her part of the line. It is of the correct period but was brought from elsewhere and erected by some voluntary wardens. The original signal at Tintern, long disappeared, had only one arm, being single-track.

We reached Brockweir Bridge, the end of her territory, and she pointed out a white-painted chapel across the river, in the village of Brockweir. 'That's the Moravians. At one time there were twenty drinking places in Brockweir and the Moravians came from Bristol to save the people of Brockweir. It's now a Baptist chapel.'

I looked around Brockweir, a nicely shaped village, round and solid, with some handsome houses, less touristy than Tintern. It has a Rhineland feeling to it which I'd noticed earlier in other parts of the Wye, especially where the gorge is deep and heavily wooded. The river is still tidal at Brockweir and at one time it had a thriving boat-building industry. Nelson stayed at an inn locally with Lady Hamilton in 1802, but I half expected that. I seemed to be finding Lady Hamilton everywhere on these railway walks.

There was a halt at Brockweir in the railway days, eaten up ten years ago for road improvements, and also at the next village on the line, Llandogo. I was told that this still existed, so when I got to Llandogo, practising pronouncing it to myself, letting it roll off the front of my tongue, I went into a shop and asked the way.

I told the shopkeeper that I was interested in the old railway and he said, 'What a coincidence! Last night, instead of reading a bed-time story to my little girl, I was telling her about the old railway that used to pass our house. She couldn't believe it.' He then invited me in to talk to his own father, Howard Cuthbert Brown, who was sitting in a back parlour having a small glass of whisky. It was about four o'clock in the afternoon. 'Just done a nice piece of work, so I thought I'll have a glass. I've been Dutch hoeing.'

Mr Brown, a healthy, ruddy-faced old gentleman of seventy-eight, joined the GWR as a ganger at £2.50 a week in 1926, working on the Wye Valley Railway. 'Every morning at seven I walked the line from Llandogo down to Tintern station with my little hammer, tapping the wooden blocks. There was one every fifteen inches to keep the rails in place. A lot of them used to come out in the hot weather. Keys, that's what we did call them.

'I'd get to Tintern about 8.30. I'd meet the rest of the gang there and we'd all have breakfast together. I used to carry my bacon sandwich with me. There were eight of us in a gang and after breakfast the ganger would tell us where we were going to work that day. We looked after the line from Llandogo down to Wye Valley junction. We'd get on our little trolley, pumping it up and down, and go along the line to do our work. It might just be trimming the banks. The line would be closed if we had any track work to do.

'I remember being a bit scared the first time I was in the tunnel when a train came through. It wasn't very nice. All the other men in the gang were much older and they told me not to worry, just jump in a man-hole and close your eyes. So that's what I did do. And it was all right. These man-holes were about every hundred yards along the tunnel, just the width for a man to get into. You always knew the train was coming, especially in Tidenham tunnel. That used to get very damp in the middle and you could hear the train roaring on the wet rails.

'The engine driver couldn't see anything, of course, but you could see his little light at the front of his engine and he'd be blowing his whistle. We had a light each but it wasn't much good, a sort of can with a long spout, oil and wick it was. I remember the King George engines, the prettiest engines I ever did see.'

He was destined, so he says for good things on the railway. The ganger in charge had told him personally he would go far, but unfortunately after only a few years he contracted peritonitis and had to leave the railway for health reasons. It turned out to be the best thing he ever did because he managed to open his shop and then a restaurant. 'I had no money but people were very kind, giving me six months credit. We've been here in Llandogo three hundred years. We're about the oldest family. My people were river people. The railway took the trade off the river, and the road took the trade from the railway. I'm lucky to have a shop and a tea place, right on the road.'

His son came back in from the shop, invited me to have some tea, refusing to take any payment, thanking me for chatting to his father. It had been an unexpected pleasure.

At the other side of Llandogo village I went to call on another old man, another ex-railway employee, whose name had been given to me by the Planning Officer at Gwent County Council.

I'd written to him but had had no reply and half wondered if
he was still alive, but he was at the front door of his little
bungalow, opening it before I'd even finished knocking, looking
very smart and trim.

His name is Charles Henry Fox – like Mr Brown he insisted
on his full three names – and he is eighty-five. He must be one
of the oldest living ex-railwaymen anywhere in the country. He
joined the Wye Valley Railway in 1919, working on it for
fourty-three years till he retired (some time after normal retir-
ing age) in 1962, just as the railway finally ceased its working
life.

Mr Fox was born in Somerset and served for four years and
ten months in the First World War, in India and the Far East.
'I had a narrow escape in Mesopotamia when we were fighting
the Turks. I was with the Gurkhas at the time. I was pouring
out a pot of tea for another Signaller and this shell landed just
two yards away and killed my friend. It blew his side off. It
broke off the butt of his rifle like a carrot. Three other soldiers
much further away were killed, but I wasn't touched. It was a
miracle.

'After the war I came over to Cardiff to look for work and
they sent me to the Wye Valley. I started as a porter at Redbrook station in October 1919 on 45 shillings a week. I then
moved to St Briavels as a signal porter at 47s 6d a week. This
meant you did some part-time work in the signal-box, as well
as portering. Eventually I got made a signalman and moved to
Tintern signal-box where I spent most of my career.'

Mr Fox then stood up and carefully drew from the inside
pocket of his smart sports jacket an envelope of old photographs
which he'd got ready for me to see. 'That was Mr Sandars, the
best station-master I ever had,' he said, pointing to a photograph of St Briavels, back in the 1920s. 'He was one of us.'

There were four railway men in the photograph, three of
them sitting on a railway seat on the platform, all very precise
and orderly, arms folded, dressed and posed according to their
rank, with the fourth and most junior, the ordinary porter,
standing behind. Mr Sandars, being station-master, was seated
in the middle. Mr Fox at the time was a signal porter and sat
on the SM's right. It's just an ordinary little snapshot, an infor-

mal group, yet one can imagine them, back in 1923, proudly taking up their railway places.

The railwayman on the left was wearing a bow tie, which surely wasn't signalman's official dress, back in the 1920s. 'Oh that was Robin. We called him that because he was a right Dandy. If you look carefully you'll see his waxed moustache. He could look very bolshie. His real name was Ted. Millie! What was Ted's second name?'

Mrs Fox suddenly appeared through a door, smiling like Mrs Tittlemouse, all embarrassed in her pinny. 'Ted Smith,' she said.

'That's it, Millie, Ted Smith. This is my wife, Millie. We've been married fifty-nine years, you know. We'll get to sixty this year, then we'll have a really good blow-out.'

I told Mrs Fox that I'd just that week celebrated my twentieth wedding anniversary. 'Quite good,' she said.

Mr Fox took me through other old photographs; of the time the river overran its banks at St Briavels and the station was flooded up to the platforms; of little children on camping holidays at Tintern whom Mr Fox let climb up to inspect his signal-box. On the back of this photograph it says, 'Timothy, Christopher and Mr Fox, Tintern signal-box, Whitsun 1959'. The snap had been sent to him by the little boys' mother.

There's a photograph of a train in Tintern station with some railwaymen standing on the platform. 'Is that you with the brush, Mr Fox?' 'Certainly not,' he said. 'I didn't have a brush. That must have been the porter. I think that's me right at the end of the platform, talking to the driver.

'One day in 1925 a woman came off the train at St Briavels and said she was never going on a train in her life again. She said the driver had gone so fast he'd shaken every bone in her body. We didn't take much notice of her. But two weeks later, I was watching the train coming round the bend into St Briavels and thought, she's going fast. There was a puff of smoke and I heard the porter shout, "The bugger's off the line!" He must have taken that corner about sixty miles an hour. The limit was thirty-five. He'd ploughed straight off the line into a field. You could have driven another train past if the track hadn't been all buckled.

'I ran up the line and pulled the passengers out. They were all very scared but nobody was hurt, although the fireman was covered in blood. They had an investigation, of course, but nothing ever came of it. We all knew he'd been breaking the speed limit. It was a near escape. There were no fatal accidents in all my years on the line, as far as I know.'

Then he took out the very sad photograph of Tintern station in the snow with the last passenger train ever to go past his signal-box, dated January 1959.

'I never dreamt I'd live to see the day when the railway was dead. I wish it was here now. Do you know, the bus fare return into Monmouth is £1.32. I get half, of course, being a pensioner. When the train closed it was only nine-pence return to Monmouth.

'I've kept my old railway hat and waistcoat and I've got a railway rule book somewhere. I gave away my old railway coat to the jumble only the other day.'

I persuaded him to bring out his old cap, which turned out to be a BR one, not GWR as I'd hoped, and I took his photograph at his front door. Then I got Mrs Fox to join him, though if she'd known I was going to take her photograph, she said, she would have put on her good shoes. I said I doubted if the photo would come out anyway. (Which it didn't.)

I then went to look for St Briavels station, just up the road from Llandogo, the scene of the train running off the tracks, but came across a lot of notices saying 'Private', 'Keep Out'. The old station is apparently now owned by a fishing syndicate, which doesn't welcome trespassers. However, for the next few miles, until Redbrook, the Wye Valley Walk follows the track of the old railway, so the walking was easy and safe.

At Redbrook I walked across the old railway bridge, at least the footpath that runs along its side. The main part of the bridge itself is boarded up, which is just as well as most of the sleepers have gone. I'd hoped for a drink at the Boot Inn, on the Welsh side of the bridge, but it didn't open till 6 o'clock, so a woman watering her geraniums in the back of the pub told me, as I shouted to her from the bridge.

I saved my thirst for Monmouth, the last station on the Wye Valley line. There were already two railway companies in Monmouth when the Wye Valley line got there in 1876. Monmouth is a bustling little market town with a population of 6,000, much the same size as it was a hundred years ago, but now it has no railway whatsoever.

Henry v was born in Monmouth in 1387 and Nelson has connections with the town, having stayed there with Lady Hamilton (again) in 1802. He was later made a freeman of the town and they have a Nelson Museum which boasts the finest Nelson relics in the world. Monmouth is also proud of its connection with the Hon. Charles Rolls, of Rolls-Royce fame, who lived nearby.

However, I was looking for different historical connections, the remains of the old Monmouth Troy station. I eventually found it just outside the town, near one of the dual carriageways, with several notices warning me I was now on British Rail property, very private, though all I could see was what looked like coal and rubbish heaps.

A large black Alsatian dog bounded out to meet me and I wondered whether to venture on, then I saw two workmen swilling down some lorries, in front of what had obviously been the entrance to the railway station. I asked if I could look round and they said yes, go ahead, it was going to be pulled down anyway. The sooner the better, one added, as it would give more room for their lorries.

I wandered round, admiring the cream-coloured wooden awnings, the old platforms, the buffet and lavatories, and even an original VR post box, all of it now a jungle of old lorries and cars, oil and axle-grease, junk and debris. One of the workmen stopped mending his lorry and came over to me. I thought he was going to chuck me out, but he led me to the entrance to a tunnel near the station. 'Look at that,' he said, pointing through the bushes. I could just make out the figures 1851 carved in stone on the arch of the tunnel entrance.

'It would look really good in the middle of my mantelpiece, that would. I'll get it down some day.'

From my reading of local history, Troy station wasn't finished till 1857, but perhaps the tunnel was built first. I asked him why the station had been called Troy. 'The Romans, I suppose. They were here, weren't they?'

According to the Gwent County Planning Department, when I later wrote to them, the name Troy originally comes from the Welsh 'troi' meaning to twist or turn, which was later anglicised to form the name of the river Trothy which flows near the station buildings. They also agreed that as the station is not listed it could conceivably be pulled down, without planning permission, as it is in poor condition.

I walked down the line for a few hundred yards, to a blocked-up viaduct over the Wye, then came back to the station and took some final photographs, or first photographs, depending on whether they come out.

The next day, waiting for the Inter-City 125 express back to London from Bristol Parkway, I thought what a shame these old railway stations are just being allowed to rot, left for vandals or turned into scrap yards. At least Monmouth Troy is being used for something, so far.

Bristol's main station, Temple Meads, is of course one of the city's greater glories, but the recently built Bristol Parkway is an absolute disgrace. It's more like a cheap halt than a station, just two platforms either side, built in a grey corrugated substance, not even iron by the feel of it, windswept and architecturally barren. It looks completely jerry-built, a temporary structure, put up for some passing battle. Yet the 125 trains it serves are so smooth and modern, quiet and efficient, with hessian-lined buffets. When trains did only 17 mph, not 117 mph, they knew at least how to build their stations.

8 🚂 The Banbury and Cheltenham Direct Railway

WALKING WITH AN EXPERT AND A PINT OF OLD HOOKEY

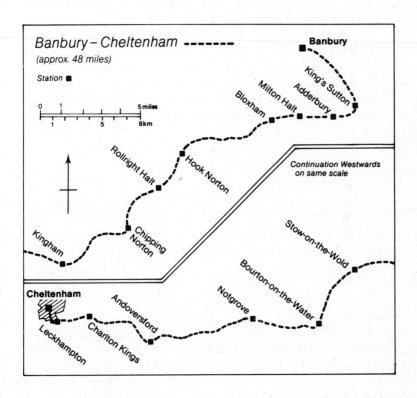

Banbury – Cheltenham ▪ ▪ ▪ ▪ ▪
(approx. 48 miles)

Station ■

0 1   5 miles
1   5   8km

Banbury

King's Sutton
Adderbury
Milton Halt
Bloxham

Rollright Halt
Hook Norton

Continuation Westwards
on same scale

Kingham

Chipping Norton

Stow-on-the-Wold

Cheltenham

Andoversford

Bourton-on-the-Water

Notgrove

Leckhampton

Charlton Kings

WE ARRANGED TO meet outside Hook Norton Brewery. As Shakespeare lovers might arrange to meet in Stratford on Avon or sex maniacs might arrange to meet on the Reeperbahn, so drinkers throughout the country know that one of the ideal gathering places is Hook Norton. I'm not a beer lover as I prefer Guinness or wine, but Mr Somerville obviously is, judging by his relish on the telephone as he suggested our little rendezvous.

I'd been in touch with Christopher Somerville for some time, though we'd never met. We are fellow members of the Railway Ramblers and he had offered to accompany me along a stretch of the Banbury and Cheltenham Direct Railway. I was grateful to have his help, and his knowledge. He has written about disused railway walks, in *Railway Magazine* and in an excellent book, *Walking old Railways*, and didn't appear at all upset by me, an outsider, moving into his province.

Railway experts are always wonderfully kind, which is more than can be said for experts in some other fields. Literary experts, for example, tend to be suspicious of newcomers, guarding their research, concealing their sources, careful with their opinions, and it takes a long time to win their approval, and most of all, their help. But railway people, they overflow, eager to pass on everything they have ever learned, happy just to have someone else with whom to share their enthusiasm.

The Banbury and Cheltenham Direct Line, greatly loved though it used to be, was always a hotch-potch of a line. For a start, the title is a slight liberty. It was true you could at one time get a train directly from Banbury to Cheltenham, a distance as the crow flies of about thirty miles, but the railway route went all round the houses, linking up some beautiful villages in some marvellous Cotswold countryside – Bourton on the Water, Stow on the Wold, Chipping Norton, Hook Norton – but going miles out of its way to do so and almost doubling the distance.

It was built piece-meal, and its many origins are exceedingly

complicated, but the earliest section was built in 1855 when a
little branch line was put out east from Kingham (the middle
point of the line when it was finally completed) to Chipping
Norton, followed by another little branch going the opposite
way, to Bourton on the Water. It wasn't until 1873 that the
Banbury and Cheltenham Direct Railway Company came into
being, and even then it took them another thirty years or so to
get Directly between the two towns. The in-filling proved very
costly, especially the great engineering works needed near Hook
Norton, and there were many financial crises and company
problems to be overcome.

The Great Western Railway agreed to work the completed
line 'in perpetuity' which in the event wasn't all that long, as
the GWR itself disappeared in 1948 and then in 1951 the first
reductions in the service began, with the ending of stopping
passenger trains between Kingham and Banbury. Its meandering country bumpkin route meant that it was one of the first
branch lines to die, even before Dr Beeching could get his beady
eye on it.

Today, it makes a terrific walk, so Christopher Somerville
had told me. He has walked fourty-four miles of it, from Adderbury in the east (the final link into Banbury from King's
Sutton is still in use, being part of the main line) right to
Cheltenham in the west. My plan was more modest – to walk
the Hook Norton section and try to capture the flavour of the
line in its old days.

I arrived at Hook Norton at nine o'clock, bang on time, but
Christopher was already there, having been inside the brewery
to ask if we could go round later in the day.

We then drove back in one car to the beginning of the
walkable part of the line at East Adderbury. It was a pleasure
to have two cars for a change. On my walks so far I'd had
endless complications getting myself back to my car, or a main-
line station, when the walk was done.

Christopher turned out to be a tall, red-bearded young man
of thirty-one whose family home is Dinder in Somerset. He had
used the old Somerset and Dorset line as a boy, on his way to
boarding school at Milton Abbey, but had hardly looked out of
the train windows, never feeling very happy that the school

holidays were over. He graduated from St Cuthberts, Durham, then did a spell in Papua New Guinea for VSO, then took up teaching. He now teaches English at a school near Birmingham and is married with two children.

It was on his first teaching job, back living in Somerset, that he first became aware of the Somerset and Dorset line, now deceased. He decided to walk its entire length, 71½ miles in six days, just for his own pleasure. His article about it in *Railway Magazine* led to a book for David & Charles and he's now planning regional guides to the country's disused railway lines.

His ultimate fantasy is to walk from John O'Groats to Land's End – using disused railway lines. One of his heroes is John Hillaby. Christopher has worked out that there are suitable old lines from Redruth in Cornwall to Inverness, covering a distance of some 1,000 miles. He changes his exact route periodically, as he researches another line which he thinks will fit into his scheme. He estimates he can manage almost three-quarters of the entire route by using old lines. The only problem is time and money. He thinks it will take him six months and cost him £2,000 in bed and breakfasts.

He's a gentleman of many talents, some of them very useful when walking old lines, such as knowledge of botany. He says this is a bit of a cheat as he's picked up what he knows from his wife who studied botany at Durham. He can draw and sketch. I suggested that if he did his own maps and drawings for his region-by-region disused-railway guide, he could do for railway walkers what Wainwright has done for fell walkers. Wainwright is also one of his heroes.

He's also a folk singer, playing in a group called Butterfingers, which may not seem an obvious asset when railway walking but it provided a very jolly beginning as we set out from East Adderbury in bright sunshine to walk to Hook Norton.

When he wasn't suddenly falling to his knees to grasp some unsuspecting flower, though never of course picking them, and then explaining to me its name and history, he was bursting into loud railway songs. He always tries to find a suitable railway song for every walk. At the opening of almost every nineteenth-century railway company, amidst the brass bands and fireworks, someone usually sang a special song for the new

railway which was later printed in the local paper. He hadn't
found one for the Banbury and Cheltenham Direct but he had
found one for another local line, the Oxford and Hampton. It
went to the tune of Yankee Doodle Dandy.

The Oxford and Hampton Railway

O come and listen to me song
And I will not detain you long
About the folks, they all did throng
Along the Oxford Railway.

CHORUS: *Ri-fan, Ti-fan, mirth and fun –*
Don't you wonder how it's done?
Carriages without horses run
On the Oxford and Hampton Railway!

And to go along the line,
Mother, father, son and daughter,
Going along at one o'clock
By fire, by steam and water.

And from the villages and towns
Ladies and gents all gathered round,
And music through the air did sound
Along the Oxford Railway.

Now an old girl looking up the line
Said, 'I don't give a farthing,
For they've pulled down me cottage fine,
And taken away me garden.

Where I for many years did dwell
Growing cabbages and potatoes;
But worse than that, my daughter now
Run off with a navigator.'

Christopher has sung his way along fifty different lines so far,
a distance of some 700 miles, though he has a long way to go to
equal the total of another Railway Rambler, Ted Ebury, who
has walked 2,000 miles.

Near Milton Halt, which has now gone, we came to a little
red-brick bridge completely covered in ivy and honeysuckle,

both of which I recognised. Christopher took some time explaining the difference between angelica, a tall, white-flowered weed, which as a boy I made pea-shooters out of, and cow parsley, which looked exactly the same to me. Angelica turns out to have a bigger globe of white flowers and a less hairy stem.

That tall purple stuff you see everywhere on old railways, once so common on every London bomb site, is called rosebay willow herb. I knew it well by sight, having pulled the flowers off to make spears as a boy, when I wasn't playing pea-shooters. The other railway flower, seen on every old line, is oxford ragwort. That's a yellow dandelion sort of flower.

Just to prove I don't always walk in a complete state of ignorance, I jumped into a hedgerow when I saw a flash of white and pulled out one of those pot insulators. But alas, it didn't have the GWR initials on it. Christopher then bent down to pick a little yellow bud from the ground and said it was pineapple mayweed. He squeezed it between his fingers to let me smell it. I said it smelled like lemon. He said no, it was definitely pineapple. I said it was probably auto-suggestion. He agreed that if it was called apple mayweed he would probably have said it smelled of apples.

Near Bloxham, we stopped to see a disused engine shed, built of red brick, right beside the track. It looked at a distance like a farmer's barn, but Christopher had previously explored inside and found a large inspection pit in the floor. From studying the OS 1 : 50,000 map, he'd come to the conclusion that there had once been a little mineral line branching off at this point, and this shed had housed the works locomotive.

One of the major sources of income of the Banbury and Cheltenham was the ironstone works. This area of Oxfordshire, as you can see in all the beautiful stone buildings, is rich in ironstone. The stone looks creamy at first sight but on closer inspection there are strong strains of red-brown running through it, showing the iron content. When it rains, it can often appear as if the stone has rusted.

The ironstone was dug out at quarries along this end of the line. At one time it was smelted locally, using charcoal, but then it went in bulk to South Wales to be processed. It was hoped in 1873, when the Banbury and Cheltenham was being floated,

and shares were being offered, that 10,000 tons of ironstone a
day would be conveyed along the line to South Wales. That's
what the GWR hoped, anyway, but it never really came to
pass. By the 1930s, most of the local ironstone quarries were
being closed.

One of the things about walking old railways is the constant
reminder of old industries. We tend to think, in the economic
gloom of the eighties, that we are living in unusually bad times.
It has all happened before, yet life has gone on, if only just in
some areas. Let us hope Lord Beeching is right. Out of decay
will come growth.

All along the line, Christopher had been pointing to bits of
stone which were almost red brown and newly ploughed fields
which showed the same iron content in the soil. Ahead of us we
saw a lorry, loaded with very dark brown earth, sitting on the
track as if waiting for us. We had seen nobody on the line so far
and it had been very easy going.

We had already compared notes on what to do about trespassing. We both agreed that if you come to a notice saying
'Private, keep out', then you do so, working your way round to
join the line later. If there are no notices of any sort, then one
proceeds, carefully doing no damage. Christopher had once
been seen off by a gamekeeper with a gun, when he'd unwit-
tingly walked into pheasant country. He has never actually
written in advance to ask people for permission, though when
in doubt one should. He'd had a letter recently from a Railway
Rambler who asked him how on earth he'd managed to walk
a certain line when he'd written three years ago to BR for
permission, and still hadn't got a reply.

We also agreed that whenever you are about to be accosted
and accused of trespassing the golden rule is to apologise first.
So as we both approached the rather menacing-looking driver
of the lorry, barring our path, we said as one, 'Is it all right to
walk the line?'

At precisely the same moment, the driver leaned out of his
cab and asked us, 'Is it all right to tip?'

We graciously gave each other permission, and walked on.

There are no relics at Bloxham these days, the railway station
having been cleared away. It wasn't a terribly convenient

station anyway, as you can see if you look at the map. By train from Bloxham to Banbury is a distance of ten miles. By road, it's only four miles. So much for the Direct line.

After Bloxham we came across a brand-new notice, which hadn't been there when Christopher last walked the line. It took us quite a while to work out what it thought it was trying to tell us. 'Private Property – No Right of Way. Access on foot along this track permitted subject to any other existing or future notice to the contrary given in writing. Signed P. J. Floyd. Council Secretary.'

We checked that neither of us had been given anything in writing, and proceeded on our way. It didn't even say which council, so I made a note to write to Cherwell District Council in Banbury on my return, hoping they might tell me if they had plans for the line. (I did write and eventually they replied, saying that none of the old line was owned by them.)

The bit of path belonging to the un-mentioned council began in great style, and we made excellent progress, admiring a skew bridge near Milcombe and coming upon some very fresh cuckoo-spit on the flowers by the side of the track. Christopher said it was done by low-flying cuckoos, who zoomed down on low-lying plants, spitting on them in passing, then zoomed off again. I'd always thought it was caused by frogs, clearing their throats after a hard night's croaking, but I accepted his cuckoo explanation, bowing to his superior knowledge of natural history. He then said he was just joking. Those familiar spits, seen everywhere in the countryside, are caused by insects. They land on the flowers, lay their eggs, and cover them in a protective layer of frothy, spit-like juice. Or was that just a joke?

We both jumped as we almost fell over two huge buzzards which flapped their wings and rose angrily above us. They were monsters, big enough to swoop down and take away even summer lambs. We picked some wild strawberries soon afterwards, very tart and rather pithy, which we were still eating when the path started to disappear beneath our feet and we found ourselves staggering along a deep, completely overgrown ravine. It was called Fern Hill Cutting, by the look of the map.

The buzzards had perhaps been trying to tell us something, warning us of Amazon jungle conditions ahead. We were now walking in a swift-flowing, iron-red muddy stream and were quickly soaked up to our knees. On all sides we were surrounded by a forest of nettles and thistles. I tried to escape up the steep embankment, which was a fight in itself, but at the top it was fenced off as a private back garden, so we struggled on down through the jungle path again. We discovered after half a mile that a culvert which had originally diverted a stream away from the railway line had burst, turning the track itself into a little river bed.

I was feeling rather tired and wet by the time we got into Hook Norton, and very thirsty. The brewery was closed for lunch and everybody had gone home. I bet they don't do that at Watneys. So we went to the nearest pub, the Pear Tree, which is a Hook Norton house and had a few pints of Hookey. Old Hookey, the strongest stuff (10·48 gravity) was 43p a pint that day. Hookey Bitter (10·36) was 38p and Mild (10·32) was 36p. All much cheaper than the mass-produced, gas-filled beer.

Christopher had a Mars Bar with his pint. I couldn't believe the Mars Bar. All that way for a pint of real ale, and then he ruins it with the horrible sweet, sticky, fatty taste of a Mars Bar. He couldn't get over the fact that I couldn't get over him eating a Mars Bar with his beer. Mars Bars are another of his heroes. When he went on a ten-day long-distance walk with his father in Radnorshire, along Glendower's Way, he took with him in his rucksack twenty Mars Bars. 'I looked at the map first and could see we were going through unpopulated parts. It was a practical precaution.' If he ever does his John O'Groats railway walk, he'll probably need a trailer, just for his cholesterol intake.

Then at two o'clock we went into Hook Norton Brewery. This might seem a rather disloyal thing for Railway Ramblers to do, when we were supposedly on an old railway walk, but it turned out to be the most interesting part of the whole day. The building, for a start, is amazing. It is six storeys high and looks like a pagoda made out of a Meccano set by a drunken Chinese architect.

The brewery started in a local farmhouse in 1849, using the pure Cotswold water from nearby springs. By 1872 the Harris family, who began it all, had built themselves a three-storey brewery, still in the Scotland End district of Hook Norton, and had taken over three local pubs.

In the mid-nineteenth century, almost every town and large village in England had its own brewery. In 1880 in Oxfordshire there were fourty-five separate breweries, each with different flavours and strengths of beer. Hook Norton became one of the leading North Oxfordshire breweries, thanks to the excellence of its brew and thanks to the great thirst of the locals. The building of the Banbury and Cheltenham brought an army of navvies into the Hook Norton area, where some major engineering works had to be done, and the growth of the ironstone industry, centred round the Brymbo Iron Company's works in the Hook Norton area, created further customers, all of them dusty, sweaty workers with unquenchable thirsts.

Today, Hook Norton is a large sprawling village with well-kept Cotswold-stone cottages, many of them thatched, several thriving-looking churches, of differing denominations, and a few handsome manorial-type houses. But there's not a sign of any industry anywhere. Everything has gone, including the railway. Only the brewery is left. Even then, with its strange 1900 architecture, it looks more like a museum than a place of physical work.

The brewery might well have disappeared in the sixties, going the way of the thousands of little local breweries which were swallowed up by the big boys. They managed to stave off any take-over bids but about eight years ago they reluctantly decided that they had better introduce keg beer, that fizzy stuff which no real ale drinker will ever touch. It looked like the only way to ensure survival. They actually bought the kegging tanks, and all the keg equipment, and were just about to start production, when CAMRA exploded on the scene. This stands for the Campaign for Real Ale, an early seventies movement, which quickly attracted thousands of supporters, all of them revolting against the Big Brewers and their artificial beers.

CAMRA has now become big and powerful, able to buy their own real ale pubs. They have organised such a successful campaign in recent years that the Big Brewers have now been forced to mend their ways and reintroduce Real Ale. You can now buy Real Ale in supermarkets and even in BR buffets, yet ten years ago it had almost become extinct.

Hook Norton became one of the shining examples of how a real ale brewery should look and smell and operate, using the traditional methods. Almost overnight, demand for their real ale shot up, and they were able to dispense with the keg machinery, without ever using it. Their production tripled in seven years and they now produce over four-hundred barrels a week and have four lorries permanently on the road instead of two. They have thirty-five pubs selling Hook Norton beer, mainly in the North Oxfordshire area, but their beer is available in the Midlands, especially Birmingham (where Christopher Somerville drinks it), and Coventry. It also reaches London, the West Country, and the Isle of Wight. The firm is still family-run and privately owned.

Inside, the brewery *is* like a museum. All the offices are wood-panelled, with leather ledgers on the shelves, and old-fashioned lettering on the doors. The show-piece is their 25 hp stationary steam engine which was installed in 1900 and is still going strong. The steam is now fired by oil, but that's the only change in over eighty years of service. We went to look at it straight away, on the ground floor, all hissing and spurting, grinding and chugging. The fly wheel measures eight feet and the body is painted a Great Western green. Its main purpose is to pump the fresh spring water up the six storeys to the tanks on the top. From there, the process of brewing proceeds downwards, a floor at a time, almost like an Emmet drawing of a factory. The fermenting tuns looked ancient, all of them simple constructions made of wood. You can *see* exactly what's going on. There's no plastic in sight.

CAMRA enthusiasts now come from all over the country, just to worship in the Hook Norton brewery, and of course have a few beers. The brewery has regular open days, such is the public demand to inspect the premises. An open day the previous week had attracted over 1,500 visitors and they were still talking about the village being jammed with coaches from London all day, filled with people who had come purely to look at the brewery. They charge them 50p to look round, which includes a free drink, with the proceeds going to local charities.

Despite all this sudden national interest in their historic work-
ings, they've somehow managed to carry on in the same old-
fashioned way, with no smart PR company taking over their
image, no glamorous receptionists or thick pile carpets. We
spoke to an old gentleman in a Dickensian office, expecting
perhaps that a guide might take us round, but he just waved his
arm, telling us to walk around on our own, as long as we didn't
get in the way. He said his father before him had worked in the
brewery, for fifty-one years.

'All these visitors can be a bloody nuisance, pardon my language, so that's why we try to organise these Open Days. We've
got another one in July, which will probably mean 1,800 people,
and then another in September. It's a job to get them all in.
Then it's a job to get them all out. We sell beer on the premises
on open days.'

The smell of the brewery from a distance had been a bit sour,
like all breweries when the wind is in the right direction, but
inside there were so many different, sweeter smells, all very
seductive if not positively alcoholic, from the dry, sharp, dusty
smell of the raw corn and hops to the rich, warm smell of
fermenting. Many of the various processes appeared at first
sight unmanned, then we came across little old men on the
carved wooden staircases, beaming and nodding as we squeezed
past them.

Back on the railway line, we went to look for any remains of
Hook Norton station, a busy little centre in its time, but could
find nothing. It was closed on 4 November 1963. A pub called
the Railway Arms was still there, but the station buildings had
been completely flattened. Christopher pointed to a line of
conifer trees, three or four either side of a little drive-way, which
he said was a sure sign that GWR had been there. They always
tried to give their stations a little bit of style, and protection, by
planting pine trees at their entrance.

The old Brymbo Ironworks have also disappeared, though
there are a couple of brick stumps, left-overs from the old works
which managed to survive somehow, despite being dynamited.
Christopher took me to see an old gentleman living on the site
in the converted offices, Edgar Turnock, aged seventy-nine,
whom he had met on his previous walk. He brought out some

photographs of the ironworks in the old days, when it had its own little railway line and works loco.

He also brought out some strange pre-war photographs of a local recluse called Theodore, a tramp-like figure with dreadlocks, who lived in an old hut, collecting mangles, old gramophones, broken bicycles. In those days, every village had its eccentric character. They weren't put away in homes, as they are today. Despite his rags and tatters, he looked so proud in the photographs, staring defiantly at the camera. In many ways, he was rather modern, with his punk-like, ripped clothes and tangled hair, as if dressed by the BBC's costume department. He could never have imagined that decades later his faded photograph would be taken out and studied by complete strangers, looking for signs, searching for messages.

The best industrial remains at Hook Norton are the two railway viaducts across a very deep gorge. These viaducts were a most expensive and arduous undertaking. It would have been much quicker and cheaper to have avoided the gorge and gone round the village, but they wanted to be near the ironworks and the brewery and what was then a very busy industrial village.

The two viaducts ran into each other, one with eight spans and the other with five, joined by a little island, and they were around ninety feet high. The girders have gone, taken down in 1968, so a local told us, but the massive stone piers are still there, like the pillars of a Roman forum. Each stands in splendid isolation, like a row of lighthouses, stepping stones for a giant. We scrambled up one side of the gorge and managed to look down and across the line of them. They appear to be made of local Cotswold ironstone, at least on the outside. Christopher thought the middle was probably filled with rubble. The top of each pier has got its own flora and fauna, untouched by human hand or foot for so many years, growing in complete seclusion, reached only by birds. He thought what fun his wife could have, climbing up to investigate, discovering what nature has managed to grow, all on its own.

Two navvies died in the process of building these viaducts, falling from the top, but their names are not remembered. In those days, navvies were lucky even to get a burial. The law didn't require a death certificate for a navvy till late in the nineteenth century. They were considered expendable.

An army of navvies billeted themselves in the Hook Norton district during the construction of the viaducts, and of the nearby 490-yard tunnel, bringing great profit to the Hook Norton Brewery but great upheaval throughout the surrounding neighbourhood.

A railway promoter, like George Hudson, got together the financial and political package when setting up a new railway company, calling for investors, creating a board of directors, arranging the right bills to go through Parliament. The railway company would then hire an engineer, such as Robert Stephenson or Brunel, who would be the architect of the route and its various engineering works. Finally, they would put the actual building of the railway out to tender, inviting contractors to estimate. The whole job would sometimes go to one firm, or it might be farmed out in bits, letting one firm do a cutting, another a bridge.

In the 1840s, at the height of Railway Mania, an army of some 200,000 navvies were at work on railways round Britain. They lived their lives in shanty towns along the tracks, moving on when the work moved, fighting amongst themselves, drinking, wreaking havoc wherever they went. They became legendary figures in the Victorian press, alarming the God-fearing who sent missionaries to try to convert them, as if they were sending them out to the African jungle. Thomas Carlyle called the navvies ugly and brutal. Dickens in *Dombey and Son* has a long description of the chaos created by navvies at work, based on his own observations.

Many of the contractors cheated the navvies of their wages and forced them to work in underground deathtraps, in primitive conditions with no safety devices. Navvies would often be paid in tokens which they could only exchange in the truck shops set up in their shanty towns, where bad meat and stale beer were sold, and sometimes even ladies of ill repute. They were encouraged to drink heavily as the contractors made huge profits on the beer sales. The truck system had in theory been outlawed for factories but that didn't apply to navvies, a new breed of human life which the law hadn't yet caught up with.

Many of today's internationally known building contractors, like Cubitts and McAlpine, can trace their origins back to the early days of the railway navvies, but the two biggest contractors of the day were Samuel Morton Peto and Thomas Brassey.

It was Peto's contracting firm which built the first ten miles of the Banbury and Cheltenham Direct line in 1855, by which time he had become a baronet, an MP and a Commissioner of the Royal Exhibition of 1851. Brassey's son did even better and went on to become an earl.

Peto employed 9,000 navvies in the 1840s, and, like Brassey, he sent them out all over Britain and Europe like advancing armies. They were often ready to do battle, if only amongst themselves.

One of the biggest ever battles between navvies occurred on an Oxfordshire line, on the Oxford, Worcester and Wolverhampton Railway – which the Banbury and Cheltenham line originally served as a branch line. It was called the Battle of Mickleton and was caused by a row between two rival firms of contractors. One firm had been sacked for failing to build a tunnel on time, and Peto's firm was instructed to take over. The original firm refused to leave the tunnel, so Brunel himself, the engineer of the line, organised an army of some 2,000 Peto navvies and marched by night to attack them with picks, shovels and pistols. The battle raged all day, with many heads getting split and limbs being broken, but surprisingly nobody was killed, till finally the troops and police arrived to drag the navvies apart.

Peto was not personally responsible for the battle, though he was attacked in the House of Commons for the rioting of his navvies. He himself was an admirable employer, an upright Baptist who always insisted on compensating navvies' widows on the death of their husbands (£5 a time) which not all contractors did. He banned truck shops on his sites, though he knew he could never stop navvies from drinking, even while working. 'A man has a right to bring a gallon with him if he likes in the morning.'

The army of navvies, though reviled and despised in peace time, became suddenly rather popular during the Crimean War. They were not only better organised and fitter than the real army, which hadn't fought a battle since 1815; there were more of them. In 1846, the effective strength of the British army was 160,000 – compared with 200,000 navvies.

As the winter of 1854 approached it looked as if the ill-equipped and inexperienced British army was going to collapse in the Crimean ice and snow, cut off from all supplies, and be overrun by the Russians. Brassey and Peto were called in to help and sent out a small army of navvies, only a few hundred strong, which during the winter managed to build a military railway, twenty-nine miles long, in record time, connecting the British army with their supply port, thus ensuring victory. Hurray for the navvies!

Peto was working on the Balaklava railway in the same year as he started on the Banbury line. Some of his navvies worked on both. There were even some Banbury and Cheltenham railway wagons which saw service in the Crimea.

It was strange to think of all the dramatic events connected with this old railway, now that all that remains is a few old stone piers across an empty gorge. There are no plaques or monuments to all the lives lost and the battles waged.

We observed a few more moments of silence, for all the navvies who had toiled so long on the Hook Norton viaducts, and then we went back to Hook Norton. We'd only walked about ten miles of the line that day, but railway rambling can be very thirsty work.

9 The Somerset and Dorset

FROM BOOKS TO BABYCHAM, A CELEBRATION
OF BRITAIN'S MOST WRITTEN-ABOUT OLD LINE

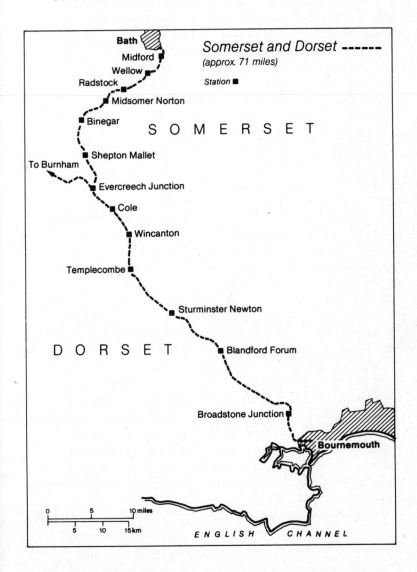

IT SEEMED PERVERSE to go to Bath just to look at a derelict old railway station rather than going to stare and wonder at the Georgian architecture, but that's what I did one morning in May. It had been a most wondrous few weeks of weather. On the radio it said that Manchester had had its first rain for forty-nine days. I thought I'd misheard till it was repeated on a later bulletin. In London we'd been similarly blessed with ten whole days of cloudless blue skies. That was why I was wearing shorts, expecting to get my knees brown over the next few days of railway walking. Instead I drove down the motorway shivering, peering out at the lashing rain.

The rain stopped for a few moments when I arrived in Bath and I considered whether I should have a walk round the streets. On my occasional and fleeting visits to Bath over the years I've always thought what a marvellous place to live, and I've seriously considered it. Yet when I return home, I immediately forget. Like a Chinese meal, the memories fade so quickly. Returning, however, there is always the same sense of surprise and the resolve to get to know it better.

But this time the Railway was calling so I didn't go to the Roman Baths, nor did I visit the Pump Room, or the Assembly Rooms. I gave the Royal Crescent and Lansdown Crescent a miss and didn't go in search of the houses associated with Pepys or Burke or Walpole, Sheridan, Dr Johnson, Southey, Jane Austen or Thackeray. What a philistine.

I did stop for a moment as I walked over Pulteney Bridge, just to look in a stamp shop window. Then I found myself inside, when I hadn't meant to. This is almost as perverse as looking for railway remains in Bath. You can buy stamps anywhere. Next I was taking out my cheque book and paying a gentleman called Mr Swindells for a Penny Black cover, dated 27 May 1840, something I'd wanted for a long time. I daren't mention the price, but the stamp did have a slight fault.

I put my head down after that diversion and headed quickly

across the town towards Green Park, looking for the old railway station, formerly Queen Square Railway Station, once the beginning and the headquarters of the Somerset and Dorset Joint Railway. It's been allowed to fall into decay since the line closed in 1966, despite endless suggestions about turning it into a sports arena or a swimming pool, a theatre or a museum. The latest scheme, so I was told, was that Sainsbury's were going to buy it. I looked in the local phone book in order to ring Bath Corporation or Bath District Council, deciding that was who now runs Bath, but all their phone numbers were in Bristol, with no listing for Bath. I decided to write to them later. (Which I did – and eventually heard from Bath City Council that Sainsbury's were still negotiating.)

The station really is remarkable. In most towns, a preservation society would have sprung up at once and mounted a national campaign to keep it for ever, but of course in a place like Bath they have so many remarkable buildings, most of them a lot older than the railway station. The local corporation under whatever pseudonym it might now be hiding, has allowed people to get away with murder. Vandals have killed off every pane of glass in the arched roof. The stone-work is dying on its feet. 'Dangerous Walls. Keep Clear,' announces a notice on the boarded-up front doors.

As befits Bath, the station was built in the neo-Georgian style, with columns at the front and a large ornate awning over the entrance. I could see no way in so I went round the side, down James Street West, and found that the rear of the station has been turned into a public car park, one of those where you put money into meters and take a ticket. They've even used part of the old platforms, and the track itself, though most of the covered part of the old station is securely fenced off. Through the fence, you can peer into the skeleton of the old station, admire the peeling pillars and rusting ironwork. I walked to the end of the car park and stood beside an abandoned red armchair and looked at the blocked-off girder bridge that once took the S. and D. over the river Avon and on its triumphant journey seventy-one miles south to Bournemouth.

I still find it hard to use the initials S. and D. without confusing myself. To a Northerner, they stand for Stockton and

Darlington. To West Country folk, the S. and D. represents possibly the best-loved line in the whole of England. Its critics used to call it the Slow and Dirty. Its fans call it still the Swift and Delightful. In the end, it became the Sabotaged and Defeated

There can hardly be a more written-about little railway line in the whole of Britain. Christopher Somerville had hardly stopped talking about it when we walked on the Banbury line. On my walks so far it had been an uphill struggle to get published information on most of the old railways. Now I was overwhelmed, which was one reason why I had kept it for my last provincial walk.

One scarcely dare approach it as an outsider, not when one hears of the books and essays which have already been published about the line, extolling its many wonders. There are lovingly produced picture books about it by Ivo Peters and scholarly prose by Robin Atthill; technical works giving you the track layout of every station; memoirs by genuine S. and D. railwaymen with titles like *Footplate over the Mendips* and *Mendips Engineman*. The line even has its own appreciation society, the Somerset and Dorset Railway Museum Trust, which, amongst other things, publishes a bi-monthly bulletin. Perhaps I should have stuck to the Georgian buildings in Bath. If I get the details of one station or halt wrong I'll have an avalanche of complaints.

The history of the line, I have to admit, is very interesting, typical of many local lines of the nineteenth century which had a bigger, more powerful brother breathing over them, in this case the Great Western. It began with grandiose plans and some magnificent engineering enterprises but ended up grovelling for help, all money and passion spent.

The Somerset and Dorset was created in 1862, a happy union between the Somerset Central which had opened in 1854 and the Dorest Central (1860). It had for long been an ambition of the local railway pioneers to create a line from coast to coast – from the Bristol Channel direct to the English Channel. The Somerset and Dorset eventually managed it.

The old Somerset Central had been broad gauge while the Dorset Central had been standard gauge. It's this sort of complication which proves of such fascination to true railway historians.

It's hard to realise now that the whole country was at one time split, physically and emotionally, over the battle of the gauge. George Stephenson, in creating the early railways, first at Darlington and then at Liverpool, had opted for a distance between the tracks of four feet, eight and a half inches. In starting from scratch, he could have opted for any width, but he chose four feet eight and a half inches, the width of the old horse-drawn colliery wagon-ways in Northumberland on which he'd first experimented with locomotives. (This width is said to have come from the width of the entrance gates on the forts the Romans built on Hadrian's Wall. A nice theory, but archaeologists have never agreed about it.)

Isambard Kingdom Brunel, however, wasn't going to copy some uncouth Northerner, and his Great Western Railway, which opened in 1838, had a gauge seven feet wide. Outside the South-West, most people thought he was simply being awkward, though he maintained he could get greater speed and safety with bigger, broader locomotives – and it is true that GWR engines were fast and magnificent, greatly admired to this day, as is almost everything to do with the GWR.

The rival gauges met head-on at Gloucester where in the mid-1840s the rapid expansion of the GWR reached the equally rapid expansion of George Stephenson's standard gauge. A lot of fun was had, by cartoonists of the day and writers like Thackeray, on the ridiculousness of everyone, with bags, baggages and animals, having to decamp from one train to another to continue their journey, just because the gauge was different. A Royal Commission was appointed which eventually decided the argument in favour of Stephenson. His gauge became standard gauge, henceforth mandatory for all public railways in Britain.

The little old S. and D. had therefore had quite a bit of expense in its previous history when converting its Somerset stretch, in GWR country, into standard gauge, but it was the tunnels and viaducts needed to get it over the Mendips to Bath which financially ruined it.

In 1874 they had scarcely got over the celebrations to open

the Evercreech to Bath extension when they announced that they were bankrupt. Those twenty-six extra miles had cost them the vast sum of £400,000. Various negotiations then took place, some of them rather devious, as they looked for a saviour.

It was naturally thought that the GWR would buy them, as they already had a line through Bath, and a station, but the S. and D. was also negotiating with the Midland to the north and the London and South Western to the south, who both fancied the idea of moving into GWR country. The Midland and LSW quickly did a joint deal, getting ahead of the rival GWR offer, and took on a 999-year lease of the S. and D. from 1875. They didn't last quite that long. With the national regrouping in 1923, the line became vested jointly in the LMS and the Southern and then in 1948 it was swallowed by BR.

When I had finally finished poking around the old station in Bath, I went in search of one of the S. and D.'s many expensive bits of engineering. It occurs not far from the station: the Combe Down tunnel, which was a mile long. It was the longest unventilated railway tunnel in the country, a record nobody could have been very proud of, certainly not the poor engine-drivers. The smoke and fumes choked them as they struggled through, especially going into Bath as the steep gradient inside the tunnel meant that they moved at little more than walking speed.

It needed a series of loops, curves, viaducts and tunnels to get out of Bath and up and over the Mendips. The physical struggles of the line, and the resulting engineering works, are well known to all S. and D. lovers. The local hills round Bath might not look very high or wild to a North Briton, but they seemed like Everest to the little locos of the Victorian era, puffing and panting, trying for economy's sake not to double head (using two engines at the front) too often. The long curves, of course, gave magnificent views. You could sit in the carriages and *see* yourself going round corners and over viaducts, which is always a thrill for any railway passenger.

I took a long time getting out of Bath and its suburbs, and I shouldn't really have tried. I knew the long tunnel had been blocked up but I'd been told the council had built a linear path along a bit of the old railway. I failed to find it. Anyone contemplating an S. and D. walk should look first at Bath Green Park Station, then head direct for Midford, about two miles outside the city. From then on, which was where the track changed from single to double, you can walk all the way, give or take a few minor inconveniences and a bit of cheek.

I parked my car beside the old railway viaduct at Midford, in the car park of the Hope and Anchor, and went in for a quick drink and a packet of crisps to start me on my way. A notice on the door said 'Gentlemen: Shirts, T shirts – but No Vests'. It seemed a funny way of categorising undesirables. I've seen pubs with cryptic instructions designed to keep out motor-cyclists, teddy boys, punks, soldiers, but I had not realised that people in vests had become the new menace.

I asked the young lady behind the bar if one could walk on the viaduct and she said certainly not. It was private. That's why a fence had been put up. She looked at my old shoes and haversack and added that *all* the viaduct land was private. Welcome to sunny Midford.

I drank quietly for a bit and then re-started the conversation with a another bar lady who looked more senior. What had happened to the old station, Midford station? 'It's now our car park,' she said. She added that she had got quite a few things from the old station when they'd closed it.

'Get any porters?' interrupted a wit further along the bar, a commercial traveller type, tucking into his sirloin steak.

'Cheeky,' said the lady. 'No, we got a few railway sleepers, that was about all.'

I went back up to the car park and studied it more carefully. The station building had completely gone but I found the platform, all overgrown. She was right about the viaduct, which goes straight from the car park, soaring high over the pub below. It was very securely fenced off. I thought about climbing over but they might have had shotguns, watching me from the pub windows below.

I knew from the map, and the books, that there were lots of viaducts ahead. I was bound to get to walk on one of them. So I came down from the heights of the car park and admired Midford Viaduct from the safety of ground level, all eight arches of it, 168 yards long. They had to make it long to get it right over all three obstacles in the gorge – the road, a canal and a stream, the Cam brook.

I walked along a road until I reached the end of the viaduct and then climbed up an embankment to look at the railway line. There was no sign saying 'Private', so I went through an opening in the fence and on to the line itself. It was broad and open, wider than I expected, with a lot of heavy ballast under-foot, as if it had been newly put down to give a solid surface. Perhaps some farmer used the old line to drive between his fields.

Very soon I came to a barbed-wire fence across the line, but no notices or warnings. I looked around. They couldn't see me by now from the pub, or from anywhere apart from holes in the ground, so I bounded over. (Once again, I can in no way be held responsible for anyone who ever trespasses on old railways. I hope that's clear.)

The next stretch was grass-covered, almost like a field, and a pleasure to walk on. Then I came to another fence across the track, marking presumably where another farmer had bought a stretch of the line. Again I bounded over, but I was now becoming rather worried. The pub lady had said firmly that the line near the viaduct was private, but hadn't said where it ended. I hurried on, watching the fields carefully in case anyone should be observing me. I stood very still for a while, after I had disturbed some pheasants along an embankment, but nothing happened. Then I heard a whirling sound overhead and looked up and there was a red helicopter, its lights flashing. Had the message gone out to apprehend me?

Until I got to Wellow, about two miles on, the next station on the line, I continually felt uneasy, in case I was about to be accused of trespassing. But from then on, all the way to Shepton Mallet, which was my planned stretch, it was easy and happy walking.

There were occasional detours to avoid new buildings and developments, or a bridge which had been taken down, but from Wellow onwards it seemed an accepted fact that people like to walk the old railway. Real railway ramblers don't do any damage anyway. They want things preserved for future generations of rambling railway lovers.

Unlike walking an official walkway bought by local councils and laid out for public use, it was nice to feel on the S. and D. that I was on virgin territory, blazing a pioneer trail, opening up new frontiers – which of course is an illusion. All the same, there is a sense of adventure in tracing an untouched old railway for one's self, following 'Cse of old Rly' on the OS map, instead of using some council's nature trail leaflet.

A great deal of Britain's 8,000 miles of abandoned railways are in a mysterious staté of semi-public use. BR and local councils own a lot, but don't always say so, neither wanting to attract nor actively repel walkers. New private owners can rarely do much with their little stretches and as long as you don't stray off the line and into the fields or break the fences, most of them don't mind your presence. The ones who do make it very clear.

Wellow turned out to be a delightful little village with its old station charmingly converted into a private house. It was the prettiest and most tasteful railway conversion I'd seen any-where, with climbing flowers and a neat lawn between the two platforms, stretching in front of the converted waiting-rooms. I knocked at the front door and waited. I could see through a window some nice old furniture and children's books and draw-ings, but there was nobody at home, alas. At the end of the station garden was a chicken run, and I could hear the hens screeching at my intrusion.

I walked up a lane into the main street of the village and came face to face with the biggest pig I'd ever seen in my life. I admit I don't see many pigs in the part of London where I live, but this was a leviathan. It was strutting down the middle of the road, huge and obscenely pink-fleshed, frothing at the mouth from its exertions. Several yards behind came a farm labourer, stick in hand, also with signs of frothing at the mouth, but keeping his distance, escorting the pig but not daring to take too many liberties with such a monster. I hurried back down the lane to the safety of the railway line.

I went over a little five-arch viaduct near Shoscombe and Single Hill but could see no sign of a halt which had once been there. A new house and garden seemed to be on the site. At one time this was important coal-mining country, which might

[151]

surprise people who forget about the West Country's industrial past. Indeed, the early affluent years of the S. and D. were due partly to the coal-mining trade. Most of the collieries had their own little branches connected to the line, but you can hardly believe it, now that all signs of industrial scabs have been removed. It seemed so lush and cosy, rich and dozy. In the distance I caught sight of a picture-post-card thatched cottage. It reminded me of Patience Strong.

Near the stretch of line I was now on, not far from the Foxcote signal-box, occurred the worst disaster in the Somerset and Dorset history. On the night of 7 August 1876, two trains met head-on and the sound of the crash was heard five miles away. Twelve passengers and a guard were killed and twenty-eight passengers injured, most of them day trippers coming home from an outing to Bath.

It happened in the dark, after the August Bank Holiday, and the blame was laid on the shoulders of the station-master at Wellow. A fifteen-year-old telegraph clerk, who'd worked a fifteen-hour day that day, for 7s 6d a week, had been left in sole charge of Wellow station. The station-master was later charged with manslaughter at Taunton Assizes and sentenced to twelve months' imprisonment. It was the railway itself which was to blame, and its rather haphazard signalling methods. After the Radstock tragedy, as it was called, they mended their ways and their safety record from then on greatly improved.

The Radstock accident is still remembered, over a hundred years later, at least by the members of the Somerset and Dorset Railway Museum Trust. I noticed in their *Bulletin* no. 97, for April 1980, an excellent little publication, full of photographs and articles about the S. and D., that one member had donated a piece of glass as a relic of the accident and that another was going to donate a wooden box, made out of wood from one of the coaches in the accident, which bears the inscription, 'In Memory of the Railway Collision, Radstock, August 7, AD 1876'.

Every bend of every disused, overgrown railway line meant something to somebody, a spot they looked for on their journey home, a movement in the train that their bodies recognised. Almost every stretch has had some sort of human drama, even though the railway workers are no longer here to tell us about it. It is reassuring to know that today's preservation societies are managing to preserve memories as well as rolling stock.

Radstock is the next station on the line, the first little town after Bath, and I arrived there just three weeks too late. The old S. and D. station, so I was told by two small boys, as I searched around the centre of the town, had just been pulled down.

I saw a stretch of real railway track and some wagons, opposite a shop which boasted 'Co-op Sleep Centre. Now Open!' This bit of line, part of the old GWR, still looked as if it might occasionally be used for freight wagons, though the fence was down and there were paths across the track and even a lollipop lady who was helping school-children on to a railway path. I walked along a bit of the track, just to feel iron under my feet for a change, and came across some railway telegraph poles that had recently been felled. I poked around the assorted wires and insulators and unscrewed a pot cap marked GWR. At last, a GWR one to add to my LMS & LNER collection from my other walks. I put it quickly in my haversack, hoping they were all asleep in the Sleep Centre.

Radstock runs practically into Midsomer Norton, the next stop on the Somerset and Dorset, and I'd read great reports of this station in its heyday, how it had won countless prizes for being the best-kept station in Somerset, if not in the Universe. I hurried in case it might be the week for knocking it down.

Midsomer Norton station was still there, and in reasonable condition, except that a modern road now hurtles right beside it and rather ruins the rural atmosphere. On the door was a notice: 'County of Avon. Somervale Secondary School. Trespassers will be Prosecuted.' The station has apparently been used in recent years as a field study centre for school-children, though it seemed to be derelict once more. The green ironwork pillars and the white-painted eaves of the original station roof looked strong enough and it would be possible to convert it still into a reasonable home, if it wasn't for the busy road nearby. Even the little wooden shelter, on the opposite side of the platform, was still standing.

The rain started in earnest once again so I went to shelter in a shed, further along the line. The main station building itself was well boarded up. Inside the shed was an old man, bending over some old machinery. I took him to be an education authority workman, perhaps sent to clear up the debris, so I got my apologies ready, in case I was trespassing on County of Avon property. At the same moment, he started apologising to me. We discovered we were both trespassers, which amused him highly.

He told me his name was Fred Targett and that he was seventy-two and recently retired after thirty-two years in Midsomer Norton as a builder. Each day now he walks ten miles, usually along the old railway line.

'I'm often asked by younger fellers if they can walk it with me but I always say no. I refuse them all. I like to be on my own. If I see something moving in the grass, I like to stop still. I might watch for half an hour, just in case. If I see a workman, even just digging a hole, I like to stand and watch. I enjoy watching any craftsman, anyone good at his job. I was brought up in the hard school. We took a pride in our work, not our wage packet. Those days are gone. Real craftsmen are hard to find, so they're worth watching.

'I'm always prepared to eat humble pie if some farmer tears me off a strip, but I rarely get chased. I've got a very inquisitive nature, you see. I've got to *see* things and to see things you've often got to trespass. I've found as you get older people don't take so much notice of you. Old trespassers don't bother farmers. It's the young people they chase. It's one of the bonuses of being old. There's quite a few, you know, if you think about it.'

He laughed to himself, but didn't elaborate. He had a bright, reddish countryman's face and was wearing an unmatching suit, jacket and trousers that had once had different partners, a brown shirt and tie. His favourite stretch of the whole line, he said, was from Masbury to Shepton Mallet.

'I like that bit because it's elevated for a long way, though there's a few cuttings. It's always better to be up than down when you're walking.'

He remembered clearly the days when Midsomer Norton used to win all the best-kept-station prizes. He took me to a stretch of the wall on the opposite platform where he said the porters built their own greenhouse, against the wall beside the signalbox, about eighteen feet long. From there they transplanted the seedlings into the station gardens. The main gardening area has now gone, eaten up by road widening. 'Each year, they always grew a crescent moon about twelve feet across, made out of flowers. It were really lovely.'

Across the road there used to be sidings belonging to Norton Hill colliery, the biggest colliery in Somerset. He pointed to it and laughed; then launched into a long saga about how he just happened to be hanging around the colliery in its last days, looking at the weigh bridge, when he just happened to acquire a heavy brass slide which nobody appeared to be wanting any more. 'If they wants it back, they can come and get it. Only thing is, they don't knows I's got it, see . . . .' And he started to laugh again.

He has found a few railway relics over the years, but not much, and he's read all the books on the S. and D., particularly Robin Atthill's.

'I did think about going as a volunteer worker at one of the railway preservation places. I went once, just to have a look. You have to have reservations about joining things at my age. They were working on a Black Prince when I arrived, trying to saw an end plate off the cylinder. They could easily have got it off by driving in wedges but there was a fellow hitting it with a 7lb sledge hammer. I was so upset I nearly cried. I turned round and left. I've never been back.'

I left him still poking around the old buildings and platforms of Midsomer Norton station and continued on my way towards Shepton Mallet.

The line soon begins to climb, as it reaches the Mendips proper. For the next seven miles or so the line goes up at a 1 in 50 gradient and this was where they were forced to use double heading, two engines at the front, or banking, which meant one engine at the front and another pushing at the back. Even so, they needed pretty sturdy engines to get them over the top.

In the last few years of the S. and D., under BR management, they managed to introduce some Class 9F locos, capable of pulling loaded trains up the slopes on their own. The last steam engine ever built by BR, *Evening Star*, completed at Swindon in

1960, was one of the 9Fs that BR used on the S. and D. run. I had admired it while up at York. It was all of course, in vain, as once again it was becoming apparent that economically the line had failed. The S. and D. finally closed to all traffic in 1966.

I eventually got to Shepton Mallet, the end of the stretch I had chosen to explore (though it is possible to walk the rest of the line, all the way to Broadstone, near Bournemouth). At Shepton I at last saw with my own eyes the prize bit of engineering of the whole line, the Charlton Viaduct. There were seven viaducts on the 22-mile stretch from Bath to Shepton Mallet, each at least 100 yards long. The Charlton Viaduct, the biggest of them all, is 317 yards long and has 27 arches. It was built in 1874 and 1883 – the second part being put up when they decided to double the track.

I stood below and gazed up, unable to count all the arches as it disappeared in the sky, curving high over the rooftops and back gardens into the town of Shepton like a huge vulture, about to gobble up the good citizens, having first of course quenched its thirst on gallons of Babycham.

The viaduct now belongs to Showerings, the makers of Babycham, who have been at Shepton Mallet for over two-hundred years. They were a little family firm, quietly getting on with the brewing of beer and cider, when they invented Babycham. The four Showering brothers launched it so sucessfully that in 1953, the first year they went national, they had to operate a quota system for eighteen months as they couldn't cope with the demand. All of those thirsty ladies, sitting sedately in the corner of the cocktail bar, turned out to be an enormous and hitherto untapped market. The rest is marketing history, well documented in the business pages of the newspapers of the sixties and seventies as the Showerings galloped out of Shepton Mallet and practically took over the world, at least a large share of its drink trade.

They're now an enormous group, part of the Allied Breweries combine, and in recent years they have at various times taken over or merged with such assorted household names as Gaymer Cider, Vine Products, Harveys of Bristol, Teachers Whisky and J. R. Lyons. Who would have thought Babycham could be so potent? Incidentally, it's a fizzy drink, made from pears. You must have seen their logo, showing a jumping baby chamois. It appears in over 90 per cent of the country's pubs and licensed premises. That's another record in itself.

They bought the viaduct for the nominal price of £5, on condition that they maintained its structure. It goes directly over their factory and gardens and is an integral part of their site. The gardens under the viaduct were the idea of Mr F. E. Showering. They were laid out in 1960, turning an overgrown swamp into a prize-winning garden, basing their design on a scheme from a 1950s Chelsea Flower Show.

Hundreds of tons of Forest of Dean rock were imported to make the paths, rockery and waterfalls. There are over seven hundred species of plants in the garden and a colony of rare wildfowl. On top of a rockery, in a Monarch of the Glen pose, stands a Babycham animal, looking out over his domain. It all has a high-minded Victorian feeling to it, an example of paternalistic pride, the enlightened Factory Owner creating an aesthetically pleasing environment for his Work Force.

The gardens cover seven acres and it takes four gardeners to look after them. I spoke to one gardener, cutting a hedge, and asked if I could get on the viaduct. That was what I really wanted to see. He said it was for employees only, but ask at the offices. I eventually found an office, knocked and went in. A group of white-collar workers, men and women, were bent over some weird-looking graphs. I never thought Babycham was so complicated to produce. I explained my purpose and they all stared at me as if I'd arrived from the moon. I wondered what sort of discussion, or what sort of silence, I had interrupted. They said they couldn't help, so I decided to explore on my own.

I worked my way first of all towards Shepton, going round allotments and back gardens, ending up in a dead end, right at someone's back door. The viaduct was towering above me, but I could see no obvious way to get up and on to it. I retraced my steps to the other side of the Showering factory and this time I got on to the viaduct, through a fence which was open.

The views were terrific, right down over the Babycham gardens and beyond into Shepton. On top of the viaduct, along the right-hand wall, there were some large, black plastic flower tubs. Showerings are obviously trying to beautify the viaduct itself, as well as their gardens beneath.

It wasn't till I was well past the middle of the viaduct, and it is a long walk, well over the length of three football pitches, curving round so that you can't see the end when you begin, that I realised there were some workmen ahead. They came out of their hut to bar my way, announcing firmly that I wasn't allowed on the viaduct. They'd left the fence open for themselves, not for the public. However, they softened when I explained I was only looking.

They were Showerings workmen, replacing some bricks. Over the years, children had been picking out loose ones and throwing them over into the celebrated gardens. Their next job was to tarmac the surface of the viaduct, so that the rain rolls off and not down into the arches, ruining the brickwork. Showerings must be a good firm to work for, I said to one of the workmen. They obviously take good care of a very costly viaduct, and lay out such lovely gardens for their workers. 'I've known worse firms,' he said, rather begrudgingly.

My last call on the S. and D. was a few miles away towards Downside School, the well-known Roman Catholic public school, where I had arranged to see Robin Atthill at his cottage home. He is the man mostly responsible through his books on the S. and D. and the Mendips, for making the railway so popular and loved.

He has been a master at Downside for thirty years, latterly head of the English department, though he is now in his late sixties and teaches only part time. One of his pupils some years ago at Downside was Auberon Waugh, the noted man of letters and dog lover. I asked if he'd ever managed to pass on his love of the local railway to him but he said no. 'Perhaps one or two of the masters found him somewhat tiresome but I considered him a very able boy.'

He corrected me, like a good English master should, when I talked about the Mendips in the plural. The correct local usage is to say you live on Mendip. There is no one hill called Mendip, just a range of Mendip hills which extend about thirty miles.

He lived as a boy on Mendip, not far from Binegar, the highest part of the line which reaches 813 feet. 'My earliest memories are of watching two 0-4-4 tank engines in their blue livery coming into Binegar station. This must have been in the early 1920s. I collected train numbers as a boy but it was for aesthetic reasons that I grew to love the line, that and the timetables. I've got an early Bradshaw here you can look at.'

He wrote a book of essays first of all on Mendip, then produced his classic book on the Somerset and Dorset line which first appeared in 1967. There have been two hardback editions since then, which he thinks have sold about 10,000 copies. It's a remarkable number, for a localised book about a little local railway. He thinks, modestly, that it was Ivo Peters's book of photographs of the line, which came out later, which really made it so popular.

'It was a worthwhile line, which served the local area, and it was significantly engineered which helps its attraction. The closing of the collieries helped to kill it off but as late as 1955 the summer traffic for passengers was tremendous. Then the car finally won.'

He still walks it regularly, as he loves to see the countryside he knows so well from a different angle, and to remember the sounds and smells of his boyhood at Binegar when he used to lie awake at night and hear the trains miles away.

He has little experience of other railway lines and has hardly walked any of the old railways elsewhere in Britain. His love, and his pen, have been solely directed to the S. and D., though David & Charles, his publisher, did once ask him to write about another Somerset railway. He felt he didn't know enough about it. He was busy the day I met him compiling up-to-date notes for yet another edition of his book on the S. and D.

Mr Atthill witnessed the final passing of the Somerset and Dorset on 6 March 1966. He estimated that over two thousand enthusiasts travelled the line that day in special chartered trains, having come from all parts of the country, while thousands more watched from every bridge and cutting. The star attraction was a nine-coach special pulled by two Southern Pacifics. The last climb, as it pulled up the 1 in 50 slope to the top of Mendip, was recorded for posterity by countless cameras and tape recorders. It was the end of steam on the Somerset and Dorset and the end of steam in the entire West Country.

The beauty of the S. and D., its varied scenery, sweeping bends and long viaducts, made it a natural for all amateur railway photographers during its last years. It had its personal character, and so did its employees. Even though it lost its legal independence as long ago as 1875, it retained its special identity until 1948. People still considered they travelled, or worked, on the S. and D., even after British Rail arrived.

As late as 1962, as a well-known Ivo Peters photograph shows, the station fire buckets at Midford still had the letters S. & D. J. R. painted on them, betraying the full and original title of the line, the Somerset and Dorset Joint Railway.

One feels rather sorry by comparison for the many other little local railways that have so quickly been forgotten, some of them just as scenic and interesting. Where are the Robin Atthills and Ivo Peters to make the Cockermouth, Keswick and Penrith equally remembered? Perhaps Christopher Somerville will revive lost memories and photographs of that and many other neglected lines when he manages to produce his region by region survey of Britain's disused railways.

In the meantime, thanks to all the wonderful books and photographs that have been produced about the Somerset and Dorset, it is one old line which should live on for ever.

10 🚂 The Ally Pally Railway

BACK IN THE SMOKE,
A PUBLIC ENQUIRY AND A HUNT
FOR A BIOLOGICAL CORRIDOR

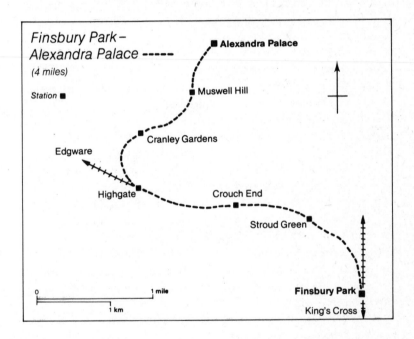

Finsbury Park –
Alexandra Palace ----
(4 miles)

Station ■

Alexandra Palace

Muswell Hill

Cranley Gardens

Edgware

Highgate

Crouch End

Stroud Green

Finsbury Park

King's Cross

0   1 mile
1 km

I PARKED THE CAR near Finsbury Park station in the Seven Sisters Road which is a rather horrible road in the urban wilds of North London. Everything seems so menacing, both people and places, though I'm sure they're all lovely, full of hidden delights, once you get to know them. There are endless terrace houses with many run-down properties, though the most run-down houses of all turn out, on closer inspection, to be hives of human industry, with rows of young immigrant workers hunched over ancient sewing machines, so intent on their jobs that they don't peer up when a stranger jams his face against a gap in the boarded-up front windows.

I stood on a little railway footbridge and could see, straight ahead, the monster main line, the direct north to south Inter-City connection from King's Cross up to Newcastle and Edinburgh. Veering left was the disused branch line, a jumble of what appeared to be tired trees, rubble, backs of houses and rag-trade factories with piles of their rubbish piled high outside the doors. The first few hundred yards of the old railway line were littered with their debris, bits of brown velvet, strewn by the wind or by kids, in amongst the bushes and the trees. It's not the prettiest way to start what Haringey Council hopes all their residents will one day proudly call their local nature walk, but it has its fascinations.

Ahead I had roughly four miles of old railway to walk on, making a steep curve round Highgate and Muswell Hill to the Alexandra Palace. It was impossible to believe there was a four-mile walk ahead, especially one part which has become known locally as a botanical corridor, a unique nature reserve, the most remarkable bit of railway reclamation in the whole of the London boroughs.

I could have ended my railway walking with something lush and pastoral, something reclaimed and converted, or something wild and romantic, but I wanted to end in a town. That's where most people live. Dead railways in urban areas are not obviously attractive. You have to search out their secrets, discover their possibilities. Most people in towns are completely unaware of them.

Haringey at one time had three old railway lines, more than most of the London boroughs, all of them old branch lines. There's a 2½-mile stretch known as the Seven Sisters–Palace Gates section, formerly part of the old Great Eastern line, which they bought for housing in 1969. It's the sort of area where you don't get many middle-class activists and they were allowed to go ahead and fill it with pockets of new council housing. They didn't intend to completely destroy the railway route, hoping to leave a walking area, but the population, so they say, 'wasn't advanced enough to take it'.

There was a vogue at the time, amongst town planners, for the idea of 'defensible space', a notion put forward in a book by Oscar Newman. The theory was that if you built municipal houses round a bit of open space, the residents would cherish and protect it, for themselves and for others who had access to it. In the event, the residents retreated into their new council houses, locked the doors and couldn't care less about the bit of ex-railway nature reserve at their front door, eventually demanding that it should be closed, which is what happened. Today, this railway route is non-existent, lost and gone for ever.

However, Haringey's other two lines, which I was just about to explore, have been saved, if only just. They now provide a continuous walk of about four miles from Finsbury Park round to Alexandra Palace, if you know where to look.

The Highgate to Alexandra Palace stretch was a branch specially built to serve the Palace, and since it closed in 1957 it has incurred a bit of development, such as a couple of schools which have been built right on the line, but there is still today a public walkway all along the route. Its survival was a triumph for right-thinking, socially minded conservationists. Luckily, in middle-class Highgate such people are not unusual.

The other end, from Finsbury Park to Highgate, is not as socially favoured. The council presumably did not expect that a rather run-down, more deprived area would squeal quite as much when it announced its plans. These days in London, of course, right-thinking people are everywhere. The professional classes have been forced to spread themselves by rising prices, colonising even the most unsalubrious of neighbourhoods.

The Finsbury Park–Highgate stretch of old railway, which is already known as the Parkland Walk, became the scene of one of the most tremendous community battles of the post-war years. It was typical of so many rows up and down the country, between local councils and local pressure groups, except that the ending was more dramatic than most.

The basic problem was that the council wanted to put up some housing on the line, as they had done elsewhere, while the local pressure groups wanted it retained with its railway character. (It's strange how preservationists can infer that old railway lines are somehow 'natural'. When George Stephenson first started he was loudly abused for ruining nature, killing trees, upsetting the game, stopping cows from milking.)

It is very easy, in all these local rows, to blame the planning departments. So, before starting my walk, I went to see Haringey's Deputy Planning Officer, Keith Gardner, in his Crouch End offices.

I had corresponded with planning officers throughout my railway rambles but had so far not met one in the flesh. Mr Gardner seemed a civilised gentleman, doubtless kind to animals, willing to help old people across the road, certainly not the baddie some of the more extreme activists alleged.

When a council buys an old line from British Rail – and the local council usually gets first offer – it's the planning department which has most to do with its future. Naturally, they get lobbied by their own housing department, by the architect's department, and by outside bodies. They have to think of the needs of the whole borough, and in a borough like Haringey, housing is always a great problem. Most of all, they have to worry about money.

'It's a very exciting prospect, to suddenly have an old railway line,' said Mr Gardner. 'In the normal course of events, you will never ever get such a large open area, up for grabs. I've been thinking of this line constantly for ten years.

'There are two extreme possibilities – you could either construct a narrow, six-foot-wide concrete path all the way along, and fill it with new housing either side, or you could leave everything as it is, disturb nothing at all, then enclose it and restrict all public access, keeping it as a nature reserve, only allowing experts in to study the flora and fauna. Those are the two extremes. In between, you have countless variations.

'We don't start with any preconceptions. We're not trying to force our will. We're a catalyst, drawing out the needs and feelings. We're here to make Haringey a better place to live in. The trouble is, not everyone agrees on what constitutes a better place.'

The first thing they did, when they took over the Finsbury Park stretch, was to ask an outside firm of consultants to look into the possibilities of the line, to see what sort of housing would be feasible. They felt housing must be their first priority. The survey, entitled 'Two Miles of Opportunity', suggested that quite a lot of housing could be built. They discussed it internally, whittled it down, argued amongst themselves, then got a second outside consultant to do another survey, this one being called 'A Question of Balance'. The title indicates that the nature lobby was already making itself heard.

The council finally announced their plan, which was to have certain parcels of housing along the lines. There was such agitation from ten local pressure groups, who immediately banded themselves together into the Parkland Walk Group, that eventually a public enquiry was held in 1978.

The Government, in the form of the Department of the Environment, listened to both sides, and finally came down on the side of the amateurs. The professionals had been beaten. They took it like men. 'We were disappointed after all the years of planning. We felt with our plan we could have met several needs, creating housing yet keeping the essential nature of the lines, but the Minister thought differently. We are now to meet just one need, but we still intend to create something of quality.'

The day I met Mr Gardner they had just received official government planning permission to turn the line, now a 'metropolitan open space', into a nature walk – until then it was still designated railway land – and they had begun to interview people for the post of Warden who would be in charge of reclaiming the line, with two assistants.

It's been a long and complicated saga, and one I've tried to simplify, but it will give hope to all pressure groups everywhere. Not many can afford the time, energy or money to take a council to a public enquiry – and then win.

During all the endless arguments over the last decade, some of the local general public, most of whom probably took little notice of the acres of grey columns in the local press, have gone ahead and used the line. Technically, they've been trespassing, but the council have turned a blind eye. Haringey have kept the eight bridges in good repair, just in case anyone killed themselves, but have done little else, neither drawing attention to it nor warning people off. The public have therefore made their own little access points, getting on the line where they felt like it.

Now that the council know what they have to do, there will eventually be a Grand Opening Ceremony, when the scruffier parts of the walk have been cleaned up, and no doubt lovely leaflets will be available for all, showing what a grand job Haringey Council have done to create a truly wonderful nature walk. Only those grey files will show the amount of prodding in the back, then eventually in the front, and finally the blood-letting that was necessary before it all came to pass. It's a story of our times.

Back at that scruffy beginning, I stood for a while on the Finsbury Park Bridge looking at some deeply embedded graffiti, 'Clock End kills Spurs Yids', wondering what archaeologists of the future would make of it. The Clock End is where some of the more vociferous supporters of the Arsenal Football Club stand and Tottenham Hotspur FC is their traditional deadly rival. The use of the word Yid is disturbing, though it has become a general term of abuse at London football grounds, hurled by hooligans at each other, irrespective of race or colour. Perhaps it is the influence of the National Front, which has become strong amongst some football supporters.

The old line starts off fairly high, with the track raised up, so you get a good view either side, looking down into back yards and back windows of the old terrace houses. Haringey officially designate it a housing action area, meaning the houses qualify for special support grants.

When you are on a train travelling an urban railway you

soon see the unacceptable face of capitalism, the reality of the daily grind, the ragged entrails that are usually hidden by a bold front. Pretences are often made with the public face, the token rose bush, the purple front door, the red-painted brick-work, even if it does stop half way, but at the back they usually give up. All human life is there, and at a certain speed, it all looks tragically the same, endless cramped boxes, endless ident-ical broken-down lives.

But when you are a *walker*, not grinding through the suburbs in a moving train, you see the human spirit fighting back, despite everything. On closer examination, each little back yard is different, as are the lives inside, though sociologists would have us believe otherwise.

We walkers can see the little breaks for freedom, the wooden shed lovingly painted in odd end-of-line colours, the tomatoes struggling to get air, the crazy paving that didn't get finished, the garden gnomes that were fussed over and then forgotten, the piles of old wood which were going to be a boat, the furniture whose face finally didn't fit, the second-hand treasures being kept, too precious to be dumped, but now abandoned, the hobbies that lasted only half an hour, the illegal extension that got started before hopes and money ran out, the dripping overflow that will never be mended, all the leaks and damp patches and running sores of urban living and everywhere the weeds and concrete fighting it out.

As I was walking along the line, slowly taking in the decrepit houses, I was stopped short by an incredible sight. Someone had turned the whole of his miserable stretch of back yard in-to a swimming pool. What imagination, what daring, what effrontery, what a proclamation of independence!

I scrambled down the embankment and could see that the blue concrete inside walls were empty, but the pool itself looked new enough. Beside the pool were some lamps, all ready for next summer's midnight floodlit swimming parties, pool-side barbecues. It may be darkest Finsbury Park, but to someone down there it was Beverley Hills.

I went round and into the street, Florence Road, and eventu-ally worked out the swimming-pool house. I knocked long and hard at the door, but there was no reply. The front path was a mosaic of different coloured bits of marble, done in a crazy paving, while what had been a stretch of front garden was now alternate white and red concrete slabs. It looked like an ice cream parlour that had seen better days.

A few doors down two old ladies were chatting at a gate. I asked them if they knew who'd put in the swimming pool. When I assured them I wasn't from the council, and wasn't going to report anyone, they finally confided that it had been put in by an Italian.

'He came over here with big ideas,' said one lady. 'Now he's sold and gone. I don't know who's there now. I saw it with water in not long ago.'

The other lady said it was nice that Haringey were at last going to do up the old railway line, but the first lady cut her short. She said the council had done nothing whatsoever. It was the ordinary people what had done it. 'I went to the meeting, didn't I?'

I left them arguing and went back to the railway.

I walked on, my spirits raised, still following scraps of the brown velvet I had noticed at the beginning, left like a paper chase. Would I eventually come to a beautiful lady in a fine flowing velvet gown?

The walking underfoot was relatively easy. The surface appeared to be beaten-down rubble, though on the verges were traces of old railway ballast. Along the embankment, the dreaded sycamores had taken over, spreading their sperm everywhere, the little seedlings growing in the unlikeliest of soils. The only railway relics I could see were concrete posts lining most of the track on either side, the remnants of posts which had carried the cables. Now and again there were big chunks of concrete, bases perhaps of signals now gone.

At the second bridge, there's the remains of an old platform, the first halt on the branch after it had left the main line, and below the bridge, peering down into the road below, a building proclaimed itself Pat's Hair Stylist. It looked architecturally as if it could have been at one time the station-master's house.

The third bridge turned out to be an iron bridge, which made a change and provided a better base for football graffiti, but beyond there were several rubbish dumps. The line had now ceased to be raised up but had become a valley, with a steep incline on either side, fortified by brick cuttings in some places. I passed a skew brick bridge and then another with a slightly vaulted roof, a surprising bit of fancy work for a run-of-the-mill bridge.

One of the bonuses of walking in a built-up area is that it is possible to work out, using an A–Z, exactly where you are, to within a street. Out on the country lines, I was often miles out. I realized I was passing Blythwood Road, a street which runs parallel with the line, so I jumped over the fence, which was easy enough as the palings were down, and went to call on Michael Radford. I had been given his name and address as one of the pillars of the campaign to save the railway line.

I thought at first I'd got the wrong house, as one window was broken, partly boarded-up and defaced with the usual Arsenal-Spurs observations, but he arrived at the front door to lead me to a neat if rather stark room at the back, where he had been working. The wooden floors were bare and the room was heated with one bar of an electric fire. There was a shelf of books beside his desk, most of which appeared to be large French dictionaries. The opposite wall was devoted completely to fishing rods. I counted seven, each carefully fixed horizontally across the width of the wall. I was surprised to learn that there was scope for trout fishing in the Finsbury Park area.

He's a tall, bearded, pipe-smoking young man of thirty-three, very precise and well-ordered who works as a free-lance publisher's editor. He comes from Yorkshire and first came to this house fifteen years ago when he was a student at London University, reading French. Now he owns the ground floor flat. In exploring the area he discovered a nice walk up the railway line to Highgate, where he could have a drink in a pub, then return to his studies. The line was still being used occasionally to move tube stock, but he worked out the times and always kept to the embankment.

One day a leaflet came through his letter box from something called the Stroud Green Community Association, saying there was to be a meeting about Haringey's plans to buy up the railway.

'I went to the meeting and it was a complete slanging match.

People were shouting "It's our land!" Haringey were apparently prepared to spend £2½ million buying it from British Rail. Most people thought it should be free. In the end, they only paid £400,000 for it, so we achieved something.'

From these early meetings was formed the Parkland Walk Group of which he became chairman, by default, he says, as someone didn't turn up. It consisted of representatives of ten different community groups, up and down the line, three of the main activists being himself, an architect called Pat Lawlor, and Jennie Cox, a landscape designer. For the next seven years they bashed away, opposing every stage of Haringey's efforts to introduce council housing on the line, until at last they were promised a public enquiry.

'I thought we would be ridiculed more at the public enquiry, made to appear a little group of middle-class conservationists, fussing about their gardens. It always was a terrible choice – Open Space versus Housing. But our point was the *uniqueness* of the line. There would be nothing like it anywhere else in the whole of London. It also provided a great opportunity to actually improve people's living conditions.'

During the period of the enquiry, the three main campaigners took five whole weeks off work, just to prepare their case and give their speeches. It was estimated that Haringey's total expenses came to £100,000 while the amateur campaigners spent a total of £9. They all worked for free of course, not charging expenses, getting friends to duplicate their leaflets. The halls they had to hire were used at Haringey's expense. (Haringey subsidises local community associations, in whose names the halls were always booked.)

'It has been a pretty shattering experience, but it's not over yet. We're still watching them. We suspect they might still re-apply for permission to build on two of the sites. We'll also watch that they don't make the line into a park, with flower beds.

'On the whole, I have to admit Haringey acted openly about their plans, though we suspected them at each stage. We thought their openness was pure cosmetics, allowing public discussion, but with no intention of paying any attention to it. That's why we're still watching them.'

Back on the line, I came to a rather strange sight, a large

stretch of tarmac and some basket-ball poles, laid out as a court, and behind it a huge wooden adventure playground, with swings and hide-outs and even a wooden theatre, right in the middle of the old railway line. Surely Haringey hadn't slipped in quietly and started developing? Then I realised I had stumbled on Islington territory. In Islington, they do things differently from Haringey.

One of the many minor complications in the saga of the railway is that for a brief little stretch the line passes through Islington. While Haringey spent ten years messing around with its consultants and public enquiry, Islington went right ahead and used their bit as an adventure playground, deciding that was the need they most wanted fulfilled.

The playground was empty. It was term time, but I'd expected a few kids to have bunked off – the London street term for truancy. The far end of the playground is an Under Fives' club and they'd painted over part of a massive brick cutting, around twenty-five feet high with twelve arches, an excellent piece of Victorian workmanship. The coats of white paint that had been slapped on didn't quite spoil the beauty of the old brickwork. Just another minor miracle of the railway age, put to a modern use.

The playground runs into the remains of what was once Crouch End station. The concrete platforms are all there, ready and on parade, waiting for trains that will never come. In the meantime, the line has become a dump for dozens of old tyres.

Just after the playground, once more in Haringey, there's what looks like an unfinished brick bridge. It's very hard to work out what Haringey thought they were doing. There are several brick fingers raised in the sky, leading nowhere. I'd passed it several times on the road above, thinking it was the wall of some garage, never realising it concealed the old railway. Underneath are some old station buildings, including a lavatory, its stalls still standing and a water pipe somewhere dripping away.

Once past the remains of the station, there is a sudden and dramatic change in the landscape. You couldn't really call the first stretch of the walk attractive, though no doubt in the future it will be, when it's cleaned up and landscaped. After Crouch

End, however, the line becomes decidedly richer and even a green sward appeared at the side of the tracks. You could almost imagine you were suddenly in the depths of the country. From now on, we're into middle-class territory. There's not the turn-over in population compared with the other end. They've always cared more for the old railway, spawned fewer vandals, repaired their fences. Thanks to having proper gardens, instead of little concrete back yards, there's been less scope for fly-tipping and a natural propagation of plants and trees onto the railway line. From now on, the most popular single tree is the silver birch. Is the sycamore a working-class tree? I also spotted some well-heeled oaks and a few affluent cherry trees.

There was a young woman walking ahead of me with her little girl, picking up twigs and little branches. I drew abreast, and they didn't recoil in horror on finding an unaccompanied male suddenly beside them, but chatted away amiably. The little girl, Alison, said she was collecting twigs to make a witch's broomstick. Walking on the old railway was her best favourite walk, better than any public park. Her mother said she loved it as well, though she'd never dare walk it at dusk. There were no lights. Haringey, even when they clean up the scruffier parts, won't be putting in lights.

The walk was delightful from now on, but I had endless fantasies of being a burglar. It all looked so easy. Over the back fence, round the bedrooms, then back into the undergrowth, lost for ever. You could have a motorbike hidden and be miles away in minutes. London's disused railways, just like their country cousins, tend to go across country in gentle curves, rather than straight in and out from the centre, which is what most travellers want. In London, it is now very difficult to make cross-country trips by public transport and even by car without first going into the middle. You have to dodge endlessly in and out, up and down, crossing arteries, avoiding one-ways and dead-ends, hoping that an attractive-looking side street won't bring you back where you started. Escaping with your loot down an old railway track could be the quickest way of getting out of most neighbourhoods.

I was faced with a tunnel and didn't know what to do. It appeared to be boarded up, but when I got nearer I found the doors had been smashed down and at the end of the tunnel, I could see light. I knew from my map I wasn't yet at Highgate tube station, which I certainly didn't want to stumble into by mistake. I gave several shouts, down the hundred yards or so of dank, dark tunnel, just to reassure myself and pretend I wasn't alone. I had told the planning people, back at Crouch End, that I was going to walk the route today, but I couldn't remember their warnings. There are two tunnels at Highgate, but one of them, they said, should not be entered.

I set off, feeling rather scared, and the first surprise was the smell. It was that old, oily, clammy, thick, juicy, rich smell of steam railway smoke. How strange to find it at its best in the middle of London, more genuine than in any tunnel I'd investigated in the country. It was in all the walls and ceiling, probably in the ground as well, so strong you could pack it up in tins and sell it to railway freaks the world over. During the 1975 Stockton–Darlington Railway 150th celebrations, I did actually buy a tin of Locomotion Steam. I still have it. Unopened. In very small type, it says on the side, 'This is a collector's item – the can is empty'. We were knowingly being conned, but the money was going to a good cause, the Beamish Museum. However, I am sure you *could* seriously sell tinned smells. Modern science must surely be able to package it. Then when railway fans sit down of an evening, to study their photographs, ogle their collection of railwayana, or run their little model trains, they could open up a tin and inhale all the memories. Railway joss sticks, that would be even better.

The middle of the tunnel was pitch black and there were some very worrying drips. I could hear a rumbling noise, and wondered whether the last train had really gone for ever, but when I got outside I saw it had been a large Jumbo, flying low for London Airport.

Out in the open again, and into fresh if smell-less air, I found I'd stumbled into the most perfect little railway station. It was the old Highgate railway station, built in the late 1930s, not connected with the present Highgate tube station which is miles below the surface.

The railway originally went north from here to Edgware. Its origins go back to 1862 when the Edgware, Highgate and

London Railway was given permission to build the line from Finsbury Park. The branch line which ran east from Highgate to Alexandra Palace was built a few years later, in 1873, by which time the Great Northern Railway had taken over.

The stretch I'd just completed, from Finsbury Park, did not close completely until 1970. There was nothing historic in Highgate station's designs or fittings, and most of it looked obviously post-war, with concrete platforms and straightforward wooden waiting-rooms, but all the same, it was as if the station staff had just moved out. Only the glass was gone from the windows. I went inside the little waiting-rooms down the middle of the platform and sat down. There was little vandalism, which showed that most people hadn't yet discovered the station, being put off by the boarded-up tunnel. The only graffiti I could read was a large chalked sentence: 'I hate Graffiti'. You get a nice class of vandal in Highgate.

In a way, the station had improved since it had been closed, becoming more attractive and less stark, concrety and functional. Down every platform, in uniform rows, were silver birch saplings. It was as if they'd been deliberately planted, rather than finding their own homes in cracks in the concrete. They stretched the length of either platform, as well as down the middle, all of them waiting patiently, natural commuters, lost in their own thoughts, standing silently for the train that will never come. It was surrealistic, a joke painting by Magritte, showing the wooden-headedness of city workers, or a dream sequence by Fellini.

At the end of the station was another tunnel, but well and truly boarded up this time. This must be the one you can't enter, that leads to the modern main-line railway. I'd come to a dead end.

One of the station buildings to the right seemed to be occupied, as I could see a child playing inside, and beside the house was a row of runner beans and tomatoes. I scrambled over the old tracks towards the house, and worked my way round some old fences, and suddenly found myself face to face with the opening to Highgate tube, with real, not wooden, commuters going down into the earth, on their way to work. The only trouble was that a ten-foot wire fence separated me from them.

A West Indian gentleman was cleaning his car in the street nearby and came across when I shouted. He seemed surprised to see me, as if I'd just come out of a hole in the ground, which in a way I had. In a deep Oxford accent, he explained how I could go back and work my way round to an exit. He couldn't believe I'd walked from Finsbury Park. He'd heard stretches were possible, but had never done it himself. He was particularly amazed by my shoes, just ordinary street shoes. Surely I needed boots? I explained that it was an easy path, all the way, dry and trouble-free. I left him shaking his head in amazement and went up some steps, crossed over Muswell Hill Road, turned right for a hundred yards, and then left into Highgate Woods.

I was now heading for the second old railway line, the former branch line from Highgate which served Alexandra Palace. The two lines almost connect, but not quite, though it takes only a few minutes to go from one to the other. The object with all railway walks is to try to keep street walking to the minimum. So far that day, despite being in the heart of London, I had avoided all tarmac, apart from that adventure playground.

I cut left through Highgate Wood, round a cricket square, to pick up the beginning of the old railway track. There's a fence which keeps trespassers off the modern railway line, but that is soon left behind. I was walking through the wood itself for some time, before realising I was already on the old branch railway. What Haringey have done, without announcing it, is to let the wood just naturally take over the old railway. It's almost impossible now to tell the difference by the foliage. Only the occasional run of concrete posts, and a slightly raised elevation, give away the old route. It is extremely overgrown and you need to do some scrambling and bending to keep on the track. I had hardly been on a more rural-looking stretch of old line anywhere in Britain.

I sat on a brick bridge, a left-over railway bridge, which now runs to nowhere, watching some squirrels playing round the base of an oak tree. In the distance I could hear shouts of children which let me know I wasn't exactly far from civilisation.

Once Highgate Wood is left behind, there is a school right on the site of the route, but the path moves round it and it is easy to follow, turning sharp left at a road (Muswell Hill Road) and under the old railway bridge.

The final stretch of the old route to Ally Pally is now well preserved as a public nature walk, with a different sort of landscape and feeling. It had been like a jungle in the wood, where I'd had to beat the undergrowth to find the concrete posts. Now, it was open park land, with little wooden tree-trunk seats, and people sitting in the afternoon sun, reading books.

I was on a viaduct before I realised it. The walkway, foliage included, just carries on, till you realise you're soaring in the air, with marvellous views over the roofs and slopes of North London. They're very proud, at Haringey, of having preserved the viaduct, and in fact of having kept all the bridges on the line.

There's another primary school to walk round, then after that you're into the grounds of Alexandra Palace itself. It is only in the park that you get the first view of the Palace. Until then, all that can be seen, even from the viaduct, is the TV mast. It is a majestic sight, a queen on her throne, as Wordsworth once said of Hawkshead church.

The railway, which closed in 1957, ran right into the Palace. You can't now walk the final few yards as British Rail kept a plot and have built themselves a mysterious-looking building which they use as a research station. The history of the branch railway is the history of Alexandra Palace, as the line from Highgate was built specifically to carry the Palace's visitors. During the year of the grand opening, eight hundred navvies were employed by the Great Northern Railway on the two-mile branch from Highgate, desperate to get it ready in time, while a hundred workmen were still finishing off the Palace and its grounds.

It was the success of the 1851 Great Exhibition which had first sparked off plans to have some sort of People's Palace in North London. The Great Exhibition had attracted six million visitors in just 140 days, many of them coming by rail, and large profits were still being made when the Exhibition hall was re-created at what became the Crystal Palace in South London.

The Alexandra Palace, named after the Danish princess who had arrived to marry the Prince of Wales, was going to be bigger and better and with pleasure gardens of some 450 acres. There had been endless financial problems, and many delays in its construction, but it did finally open on 23 May 1873. Sixteen days later, it was burned to the ground.

During those sixteen days, over 100,000 passengers had travelled on the Great Northern's Ally Pally branch, which gives some idea of its enormous popularity, and work was immediately started to rebuild the Palace. It was done at incredible speed, re-opening just two years later, in May 1875, at a cost of £417,000. The new building covered eight acres.

At Whitsun that year over 90,000 people travelled on the railway in one day, while in the first six months of its opening, 1,307,857 people visited the Palace. The following year, 1876, the Palace went bankrupt. The cost of running such an enormous building, and paying back all the loans, had proved just too expensive.

From then on, until the present day, the Palace has proved a financial white elephant for all its owners, including Haringey Council, who bought it from the GLC in 1979 for the nominal sum of £1, plus £8½ million towards its restoration.

Despite all its financial problems, the Palace has been a greatly loved object for millions of North Londoners over the last hundred years. There was a famous racecourse in the grounds where Steve Donoghue, Fred Archer and Gordon Richards rode many winners, but it closed in 1970. Blondin, fresh from crossing Niagara Falls on a tightrope, once did daring exhibitions in the park. Heifetz, Kreisler, Galli-Curci, George Gershwin and many others have performed in the Great Hall. In 1936 the BBC, who still have one wing, opened the world's first regular TV service from Alexandra Palace.

I went up to the entrance hall and asked if I could look inside. In the first hall I could see people getting ready for an exhibition of Lego models. Coming soon, so I read on the notice board, were exhibitions of Vintage Cars and Racing Pigeons, Table Tennis, Jazz, an Organ Recital, Fireworks, an Olde Tyme Music Hall, a National Exhibition of Cage and Aviary Birds, Racing Motorcycles, a Tchaikovsky Concert, a Jumble Sale.

The man at the entrance desk said the public weren't allowed in today, but I should ask at the admin offices, so I threaded my way past the Lego models and came to a side office where six ladies were guzzling cream cakes. It was about three in the afternoon, a bit early for tea, rather late for lunch. Perhaps it was someone's birthday.

I stood around, not wanting to interrupt the eating, till one of them, wiping cream from her lips, asked what I wanted. I enquired if they had a book I could buy about the history of the Palace, but it was sold out.

I said I was mostly interested in looking at the old railway station, part of the Palace building, as I'd just walked the railway. Two of the ladies stopped guzzling and came to peer at my map, working out how on earth I'd managed it. They suggested I find one of the security men and talk him into taking me down, which I did.

He took me to the Palace's old railway station which I was surprised to find was structurally intact, still with the old wooden banister rails down the stone steps, the little booking hall with its windows, the original platforms and around the walls the remains of some old railway posters.

Then we squeezed through some stone arches, under the floor of the great hall. 'You're supposed to hear the ghost under here,' he said. 'We're under the skating rink now. This old bloke died, but comes back to haunt the ice at night, so they say. I've never heard it. Just a publicity gimmick, if you ask me.'

Alas for the ghost, and the skating rink. Not long after my tour of the Alexandra Palace, which I now realise was quite an historic little visit, the Palace suffered its second great fire. In July 1980, two-fifths of it was destroyed in a blaze, including the Great Hall and the skating rink. At the time of writing, it is not clear what Haringey Council are going to do with it, though they have promised that a new leisure complex will rise once again from the ashes.

The old railway station underneath has apparently not been damaged. On my visit I had noticed that the original platforms from the first station, before the first fire, had also survived. There is obviously a lot of scope there, if someone wants to incorporate a railway museum in the new plans for the Palace, or even to open up the branch railway once again.

In the old days, the million or so visitors who travelled every year from Central London to visit the Palace and its grounds could get there by train in fifteen minutes. The normal journey by car today is much longer, and far more expensive.

We must presume, however, that branch railways have been killed for ever, which was a local tragedy at the time in almost every region affected, but out of their ashes has come a new leisure activity, not at all complex, one that anyone can follow, given a gentle bit of map reading.

When the new Alexandra Palaces rises once again, try walking to it along the old railway from Highgate, or even from Finsbury Park, now that that stretch is being cleaned up. Londoners are lucky to have such a walk on their very doorstep.

No matter where you live in Britain, there is an old disused railway line not very far away, overgrown perhaps, probably overlooked, certainly undervalued. They are unique botanical corridors, treasure trails full of local historical, social, industrial and architectural interest, all of them just waiting to be explored.

Appendices

APPENDIX 1 Disappearing Railways

In 1923, Britain's 124 different railway companies merged themselves into four main companies – the event known as 'grouping'. This is the number of route miles the Big Four then controlled:

London, Midland and Scottish (LMS)	7,370	miles
London and North Eastern Railway (LNER)	6,676	,,
Great Western Railway (GWR)	3,203	,,
Southern Railway (SR)	2,114	,,

On 1 January 1948, when all the railway companies became nationalised and a government monopoly, British Rail, took over, the total number of route miles was very much the same, around 19,000. Since then the total has fallen dramatically, especially after the Beeching Report of 1963:

1947	19,639
1955	19,061
1960	18,143
1964	15,991
1967	13,172
1972	11,444
1977	11,168
1979	11,020
1981	11,000

By January 1981, British Rail had closed 8,030 railway miles – 6,716 miles had been sold and 1,314 miles were either for sale or to be disposed of in the future.

In 1947 there were approximately 7,000 railway stations. In 1980, there were 2,365.

Appendix 2 Chapter Notes (further information, addresses, publications)

Chapter 1 Three Bridges to East Grinstead, 'Worth Way'
Six miles long, open for walking, cycling, horse-riding. Leaflet available from West Sussex County Council, County Hall, Chichester.

The walk can be continued into East Sussex along the Forest Way which is 9½ miles long and also open to walkers, cyclists and horses. It runs from East Grinstead to Groombridge. Leaflet available, price 15p, from East Sussex County Council, County Estates Surveyor, Lewes.

Chapter 2 London to Leicester, Great Central Railway
Originally 82 miles long – about 60 miles of it can be walked, though no leaflets available.
Railway Ramblers: Secretary Nigel Willis, 11 Milverton Avenue, Leicester.
Preservation Society: Great Central Railway (Main Line Steam Trust Ltd), Great Centre Road, Loughborough.
Book: *Main Line Lament* by Colin Walker, Oxford Publishing Co., 1973.
Railway Philatelic Group: Peter Johnson, 218 Blue Gates Road, Leicester.

Chapter 3 Pocklington to York
Books and booklets:
 Railway History and the Local Historian, by E. H. Fowkes, E. Yorks Local History Society, 1963
 Beginnings of the East Yorks Railways, by K. A. Macmahon, E. Yorks L. H. Soc., 1953
 Yorkshire Railways, by A. Haigh and David Joy, Dalesmen, 1979
 This is York, edited by Michael Harris, Ian Allen, 1980.
Pocklington School, Pocklington, York (Pocklington 3125).
National Railway Museum, Leeman Road, York (York 21261).

Chapter 4 Deeside Line – Aberdeen to Ballater
Leaflet: *The Old Deeside Line Walk*, available from Dept of Leisure, City of Aberdeen, Broad Street, Aberdeen.
Books and booklets:
 Stories of Royal Deeside's Railway, by A. Derek Farr, Kestrel, 1971
 Royal Journey, by C. Hamilton Ellis, BR, London, 1964

Disused Railway Lines in Scotland, by Edward Parham, Countryside Commission for Scotland, 1972
History of the Great North of Scotland Railway, by Sir Malcolm Barclay-Harvey, Locomotive Publishing Co., 1949 (out of print)
Great North of Scotland Railway Association: Secretary, 14 Gordon Road, Bridge of Don, Aberdeen.

CHAPTER 5 COCKERMOUTH-KESWICK-PENRITH
Books and booklets:
    Old Lakeland Transport, by Irvine Hunt, Rusland Press, 1978
    Railways of Cumbria, by Peter W. Robinson, Dalesman, 1980
    History of the Cockermouth, Keswick and Penrith Railway, by W. Mc-Gowan Gradon, 1948 (out of print)
Cumbrian Railways Association: Secretary Ken Ormrod, 13 Wattsfield Avenue, Kendal, Cumbria.
Lake District National Park: Special Planning Board, Busher Walk, Kendal.
Allendale District Council: Town Hall, Cockermouth.

CHAPTER 6 THE WIRRAL WAY
Leaflets, Nature Trails, Teachers' Packs, Information, etc., available from Wirral Country Park, Station Road, Thurstaston, Wirral, Merseyside (Phone: 051-648-4371). This is also the address of the Visitor Centre.
Books:
    This is Parkgate, by Geoffrey Place, Parkgate and District Society, 1979
    The Dee Estuary, by Dee Estuary Conservation Group, 1976

CHAPTER 7 THE WYE VALLEY
Leaflet: *Lower Wye Valley Walk*, from County Planning Officer, County Hall, Cwmbran, Gwent
Books and booklets:
    Tintern Abbey, by D. E. Craster, HMSO, 1976
    Monmouth and its Railways, Stephenson Locomotive Society, 1959
    Offa's Dyke Path, by Christopher John Wright, Constable, 1976
Tintern Station Visitor Centre, Tintern, Gwent
Offa's Dyke Association, Old School House, Knighton, Powys

CHAPTER 8 BANBURY TO CHELTENHAM
Book: *Chiltern and Cotswolds*, by R. Davies and M. D. Grant (Forgotten Railways series), David & Charles, 1975
Hook Norton Brewery, Hook Norton, Banbury.

CHAPTER 9 THE SOMERSET AND DORSET
Books:
> *The Somerset and Dorset Railway*, by Robin Atthill, David & Charles (new ed. 1980)
> *The Somerset and Dorset*, by Ivo Peters, Oxford Publishing Co., 1974
> *The S. & D. Railway*, by D. S. Barrie and C. R. Clinker, Oakwood Press, 1978
> *Mendips Engineman*, by P. W. Smith, Oxford Publishing Co., 1972
> *Footplate over the Mendips*, by P. W. Smith, Oxford Publishing Co., 1978

Somerset and Dorset Railway Museum Trust, Washford Station, Minehead, Somerset (bi-monthly bulletin).

CHAPTER 10 ALEXANDRA PALACE
Books:
> *Rails to the People's Palace*, by Reg Davies, Hornsey Historical Society, 1980
> *Alexandra Park and Palace*, by Ron Carrington, GLC, 1975

APPENDIX 3 Other Useful Books and Publications

Christopher Somerville, *Walking Old Railways*, David & Charles, 1979
Gareth Lovett Jones, *Railway Walks*, Pierrot, 1980
Terry Coleman, *The Railway Navvies*, Penguin, 1970
Regional History of the Railways of Great Britain series, David & Charles (12 volumes)
Forgotten Railway series (David & Charles):
  Chilterns and Cotswolds, by R. Davies and M. D. Grant
  East Anglia, by R. S. Joby
  East Midlands, by P. Howerd Anderson
  North and Mid Wales, by Rex Christiansen
  North and East England, by K. Hoole
  Scotland, by John Thomas
  South-East England, by H. P. White
  North-West England, by John Marshall

F. G. Cockman, *Lost Railways*, Shire Publications, 1980.
Dr J. H. Appleton, *Disused Railways in the countryside of England and Wales* (Report to the Countryside Commission), HMSO, 1970

APPENDIX 4 Other Useful Addresses

Commons, Open Spaces and Footpaths Preservation Society, 166
Shaftesbury Avenue, London, WC2 (836 7220).

The Ramblers' Association, 1–5 Wandsworth Road, London, SW8
(582 6878).

Railway Magazine, Dorset House, Stamford Street, London, SE1.

Countryside Commission, John Dower House, Crescent Place,
Cheltenham.

Countryside Commission for Scotland, Battleby, Redgorton, Perth.

British Rail Property Board, 274 Bishopsgate, London EC2.

Branch Line Society, 15 Springwood Hall Gardens, Gledholt,
Huddersfield, Yorkshire.

APPENDIX 5 Converted Railways

Disused railway lines in England, Wales and Scotland which are officially open to the public as footpaths, walkways or nature trails. In some cases, although the local council has bought ex-railway land for public use, only short stretches have so far been formally opened. Further and more up-to-date information should be obtained from the local authority. The local planning officer is normally the best person to approach.

There are of course several thousand miles of other disused railways, nominally in private hands (usually adjacent landowners), on which access is often unofficially permitted, but local enquiries and permissions will have to be dealt with personally.

AVON
Radstock–Midsomer Norton, two-mile footpath along Somerset and Dorset
Bitton–Bath, cycleroute, 5 miles (for details, contact *Cyclebag*, 35 King Street, Bristol)
Yatton–Cheddar, Cheddar Valley Railway Walk, 10 miles (negotiations still going on, but can already be walked)
Lyncombe Vale Nature Trail, between Devonshire and Combe Down Tunnels, Bath, ¾ mile (Somerset and Dorset line)

BEDFORDSHIRE
Stevington – nature trail, 1½ miles

BUCKINGHAMSHIRE
Wolverton–Newport Pagnall, footpath and cycleway, 3 miles

CHESHIRE
Whitegate Way–Winsford, 6 miles

CLEVELAND
Hartburn–Hardwick, 3 miles
South Bank–Normanby, 1½ miles

CORNWALL
Wadebridge–Padstow, 6 miles

CUMBRIA
Workington – 2 miles along Penrith line
Keswick–Threlkeld, 3 miles
Public footpath near Roosecote Sands (site of special scientific interest) on Piel branch, 1 mile

DERBYSHIRE
Cromford–Buxton, High Peak Trail, 17½ miles
Ashbourne–Parsley Hay, Tissington Trail, 13 miles
Hayfield–New Mills, Sett Valley Trail, 13 miles
Rowsley–Blackwell Mill, Buxton, 9 miles of old Midland Railway (just bought by Peak Planning Board, to be a public walkway)

DEVON
Tipton St John's–Bowd (Sidmouth branch), 1½ miles
Plym Bridge–Bickleigh (GWR Plymouth–Launceston branch), 2 miles
Barnstaple–Braunton, 3 miles
Yelverton–Princetown, 10½ miles
Bovey Tracey–Lustleigh (Moretonhampstead branch), 1½ miles

DORSET
Blandford Forum–Sturminster Marshall, bridleway along part of Somerset and Dorset, 5 miles

DURHAM
Consett–Swalwell, Derwent Walk, 10½ miles
Consett–Waskerley, Waskerley Way, 7 miles
Durham City–Bishop Auckland, Bishop Brandon Walk, 9½ miles
Durham City–Crook, Deerness Valley Walk, 9 miles (Durham County Council has bought 70 miles of railway lines; contact planning officer for latest details of public walkways)

ESSEX
Brightlingsea–Wivenhoe, 3 miles

GLOUCESTERSHIRE
South Cerney, Cotswold Water Park, 1½ miles

HAMPSHIRE
Litchfield–Highclere, 3 miles
Knowle Junction–West Meon, 9 miles

HERTFORDSHIRE
Hertford–Cole Green, Cole Greenway, 4 miles
Wheathampstead–Welwyn Garden City, Ayot Greenway, 4 miles

HUMBERSIDE
Market Weighton–Cherry Burton, 9 miles
Hull–Skirlaugh, 13 miles

ISLE OF WIGHT
Shanklin–Wroxall, 2½ miles
Yarmouth–Freshwater, 2½ miles

LANCASHIRE
Glasson Dock–Aldcliffe, Lune Estuary Footpath, 3½ miles
Eccles–Tyldesly–Wigan (sections walkable)

LEICESTERSHIRE
Shenton Station–Ashby de la Zouch canal, 1 mile

LINCOLNSHIRE
Horncastle–Woodhall Spa, Spa Trail, 7 miles (part of Viking Way
   long-distance footpath)

LONDON
Highgate–Alexandra Palace, Parkland Walk, 2 miles
Finsbury Park–Highgate, 2 miles
Harrow–Wealdstone–Stanmore, 1¾ miles

MANCHESTER (GREATER)
Chorlton Junction–Heaton Mersey, 1½ miles
Stalybridge–Millbrook, 1 mile

MERSEYSIDE (AND CHESHIRE)
West Kirby–Hooton, Wirral Country Park, 12 miles

NOTTINGHAMSHIRE
Farnsfield–Southwell, Southwell Trail, 4½ miles

SHROPSHIRE
Coalport–Telford, Silkin Way, 4 miles
Coalport–Ironbridge, South Bank Footpath, 3 miles

STAFFORDSHIRE
Stoke on Trent, Greenways Loop Line through the city for walkers, cyclists, horse riders, 3 miles
Waterhouses–Hulme End, Manifold Valley, 8½ miles

SUFFOLK
Hadleigh–Raydon, 2½ miles
Haverhill, Railway Walk through the town, 3 miles
Lavenham, 1½ miles
Long Melford, 1 mile
Sudbury–Rodbridge, Valley Walk, 2 miles
Southwold–Blythburgh, 3½ miles

SUSSEX, EAST
East Grinstead–Groombridge, Forest Way, 9 miles
Heathfield–Polgate, Cuckoo Walk, 10 miles

SUSSEX, WEST
East Grinstead–Worth, Worth Way, 6 miles
Shoreham–Baynards, 18 miles

TYNE AND WEAR
Consett–Swalwell, Derwent Way (shared with Durham), 10½ miles

WEST MIDLANDS
Aldersley–Castlecroft, Valley Park, 3 miles
Harborne Trail, 2 miles
Kingswinford Branch, 7 miles

YORKSHIRE (NORTH)
Ingleby Greenhow–Farndale Moor, Lyke Wake Walk, 6½ miles
Scarborough–Hawkser, 13 miles

WALES

GLAMORGAN (MID)
Dare Valley–Cwmaman, 3 miles

GLAMORGAN (WEST)
Glyncorrwg–Cymmer, 3 miles
Cymmer–Blaengwynfi, 3 miles

APPENDIX 5

GWENT
Redbrook–Whitebrook, 2 miles (part of Wye Valley Walk)

GWYNEDD
Penmaenpool–Arthog, 4 miles

POWYS
Govilon–Llanfoist, 3 miles

SCOTLAND

CENTRAL REGION
Alloa–Dollar (proposed walkway), 5 miles

DUMFRIES AND GALLOWAY
Gatehouse–Mossdale, 10 miles (part of Dumfries–Stranraer Railway, now owned by council, un-converted, but open to walkers)

FIFE
St Andrews–Leuchars, 4½ miles
St Andrews–Leven, 25 miles approx.
Boblingen Way, Glenrothes New Town, 2 miles approx.

GRAMPIAN
Aberdeen–Culter, Deeside line, 8 miles
Cambus O'May–Ballater, Deeside line, 4 miles

HIGHLAND
Ballindalloch–Dufftown, Speyside Walkway, 16 miles (with more to come)

LOTHIAN
Kirkliston–Lochend, Edinburgh, 5 miles
Edinburgh–Dalkeith, Waverley line (proposed)
Slateford–Juniper Green nature trail (3 miles)
Elphinstone–Saltoun, Pencaitland Railway Walk, 5 miles

STRATHCLYDE
Kelvin Railway Bridge, Glasgow, part of Kelvin Way
Lochearnhead–Dunblane, 25 miles approx.
Kippen–Stirling, 10 miles
Crosshouse–Cunningham, Kilmarnock, 7 miles approx.

Index

INDEX

INDEX